WILLIAM BLAKE

PAINTER AND POET

The Sons of God. Design from the Book of Job.

WILLIAM BLAKE

PAINTER AND POET

By

RICHARD GARNETT, LL.D.

Keeper of the Printed Books in the British Museum

HASKELL HOUSE PUBLISHERS LTD.

Publishers of Scarce Scholarly Books

NEW YORK, N. Y. 10012

1971

First Published 1895

HASKELL HOUSE PUBLISHERS LTD.
Publishers of Scarce Scholarly Books
280 LAFAYETTE STREET
NEW YORK, N. Y. 10012

Library of Congress Catalog Card Number: 77-115857

Standard Book Number 8383-1074-5

Printed in the United States of America

LIST OF ILLUSTRATIONS

PLATES

ILLUSTRATIONS IN THE TEXT

WILLIAM BLAKE

CHAPTER I

Preliminary observations—Blake's Birth—Education—Marriage—Early Poems—Drawings and Engravings.

THE position of William Blake among artists is exceptional. Of no other painter of like distinction, save Dante Rossetti, can it be said that his fame as a poet has fully rivalled his fame as a painter; much less that, in the opinion of some, his fame as a seer ought to have exceeded both. Many painters, from Reynolds downwards, have written admirably upon art; in some instances, notably Haydon's, the worth of their precepts greatly exceeds that of their performance. But, Rossetti always excepted, perhaps no other painter of great distinction, save Michael Angelo alone, has achieved high renown in poetry, and the compass of Michael Angelo's poetical work is infinitesimal in comparison with his work as an artist. Again, the literary achievements of an Angelo or a Reynolds admit of clear separation from their performances as artists. The critic who approaches them from the artistic side may, if he pleases, omit the literary side entirely from consideration. This is impossible with Blake, for not only do the artistic and the poetical monuments of his genius nearly balance each other in merit and in their claim upon the attention of posterity, but they are the offspring of the same creative impulse, and are indissolubly fused together by the process adopted for their execution. A study of Blake, therefore, must include more literary discussion than would be allowable in a monograph on any other artist. The poet and painter in Blake, moreover, are but manifestations of the more comprehensive character of seer, which suggests inquiries alien to both these arts ; while the personal character of the man is so fascinating, and his intellectual character so perplexing, that the investigation of either of them might afford, and often has afforded, material for a prolonged discussion. In the following pages it will be our object, whenever compelled to quit the safe ground of biographical narrative, to subordinate all else to the consideration of Blake as an artist; but the Blake of the brush is too emphatically the Blake of the pen to be long dissociated from him, and neither can be detached from the background of abnormal visionary faculty.

From a certain point of view, artists may be regarded as divisible into three classes : those who regard the material world as an unquestionable solid reality, whose accurate representation is the one mission of Art ; those to whom it is a mere hieroglyphic of an essential existence transcending it ; and those who, uniting the two conceptions, are at the same time idealists and realists. The greatest artists generally belong to the latter class, and with reason, for a literal adherence to matter of fact almost implies defect of imagination ; while an extravagant idealism may be, to say the least, a convenient excuse for defects of technical skill. It is difficult to know whether to class the works of the very greatest artists as realistic or idealistic. Take Albert Dürer's *Melancholia*. It is a hieroglyph, a symbol, an expression of something too intense to be put into words ; a delineation of what the painter beheld with the inner eye alone. Yet every detail is as correct and true to fact as the most uninspired Dutchman could have made it. Take Titian's *Bacchus and Ariadne*, and observe how separate details which the artist may have actually noticed, are combined into a whole which has never been beheld, save by the spiritual vision, since the last thyrsus was brandished by the last Mænad. Yet, though the creators of such scenes are the greatest, some realists, such as Velasquez, have in virtue of surpassing technical execution asserted a nearly equal rank. The case is different when we come to the enthusiasts and visionaries, whose art is wholly symbolic, who have given us little that can be enjoyed as art for art's sake, without reference to the ideas of which it is made the vehicle. In many very interesting artists, such as Wiertz and Calvert and Vedder, and in many isolated works of great masters, such as Giorgione's *Venetian Pastoral*, the feeling is so much in excess of the execution—admirable as this may be—that the result is rather a poem than a picture. But only one artist who has deliberately made himself the prophet of this tendency, who has avowedly and defiantly discarded all purpose from his works save that of spiritual suggestiveness, seems to have ever been admitted as a candidate for very high artistic honours, and he is our countryman, William Blake.

This circumstance alone should render Blake an interesting object of study, even for those who can see no merit in his works: indeed, the less the merit the more remarkable the phenomenon. He is, moreover, a most peculiar and enigmatical character, both intellectually and morally. As an art critic he is of all the most dogmatic, trenchant, and revolutionary. As a poet, were nineteen-twentieths of his compositions to be discarded as rubbish, lyrics would remain not only exquisite in themselves, but possessing the incommunicable and Sapphic quality that a single stanza, even a single phrase, would often suffice to make the writer immortal. The question of his sanity is as well adapted to furnish the world with an interminable subject of discussion as the execution of Charles I. or the assassination of Cæsar. Finally, it is very significant that while no man ever wilfully put more obstacles into the way of his success than Blake, whether as artist, thinker, or poet, and he did in fact succeed in condemning himself to poverty and obscurity, the verdict of his contemporaries is now so far reversed that the drawings which a kind friend overpaid, as he thought, at fifty guineas, are worth a thousand pounds.

What manner of man was he to whose shade the world has made this practical apology?

William Blake was born on November 28th,[1] 1757, at 28, Broad Street, Golden Square. By a singular coincidence this was the very year which a still more celebrated mystic, Swedenborg, had announced as that of the Last Judgment in a spiritual sense, which was by no means to preclude the world from going on in externals pretty much as usual. Blake's father, James Blake, was a hosier in moderately prosperous circumstances, whose father is stated by Blake's most elaborate commentators, Messrs.

[1] November 20 has been stated as the date, but the above is shown to be correct by the horoscope drawn for November 28, 7.45 P.M. in *Urania, or the Astrologer's Chronicle*, 1825, published therefore in Blake's lifetime, and undoubtedly derived from Varley.

Ellis and Yeats, to have been originally named O'Neil, and to have assumed his wife's name as a means of escape from pecuniary difficulties. This wife, however, was not the mother of James. This genealogy is not supported by any strong authority, and is at variance with another, also indifferently supported, according to which the artist's family were connected with the admiral's. We must leave the question where we find it, merely remarking that Blake's parents were certainly Protestants, and that we can detect no specifically Irish trait in his character or his works. He had three brothers—one, James, mild and unassuming like his father; another, Robert, who died young, apparently with more affinity to William; the third, John, a scapegrace. There was also a sister who never married, and is described as a thorough gentlewoman, reserved and proud. None of the family except William and Robert seem to have shown any artistic talent. With William it must have been precocious, for, ere he had attained the age of ten, his father, who as a small tradesman might rather have been expected to have thwarted the boy's inclinations, placed him at "Mr. Pars' drawing school in the Strand." Here he learned to draw from plaster casts—the life was denied him—and with the aid of his father and a friendly auctioneer collected prints, then to be picked up cheap, showing from the very first, as he afterwards related, a complete independence of the pseudo-classic taste of the day. At four he had had his first vision, when "God put his forehead to the window, which set him screaming." At eight or ten he saw a tree filled with angels, and angelic figures walking among haymakers. "The child is father to the man."

At the age of fourteen Blake was apprenticed to the engraver Basire. Ryland had been thought of, but Blake, according to a story which he must have narrated, but may not improbably have imagined, demurred, declaring that the fashionable engraver looked as if he would one day be hanged, as he actually was. Basire's practice lay chiefly in engraving antiquities, and the last five years of Blake's apprenticeship were chiefly spent in drawing tombs and architectural details in Westminster Abbey a most advantageous discipline, which imbued his mind with the Gothic spirit, an influence already in the air, evincing itself in Götz von Berlichingens, Rowley Poems, Percy Relics, and Castles of Otranto; and, by directing him to English history and Shakespeare, powerfully stimulated and felicitously guided the poetical genius of which he was shortly to give proof. He drew, Malkin tells us, the monuments of kings and queens in every point of view he could catch, frequently standing on them. The heads he considered as portraits, and all the ornaments appeared as miracles of art to his Gothicised imagination. Nor could a better environment for a mystic be desired than the venerable and generally solitary temple, "the height, the space, the gloom, the glory," with its music, its memories, and its constant sense of the presence of the dead. The bent of his mind at the time is shown by his first engraving, *Joseph of Arimathea among the Rocks of Albion*, copied, as he states, from a scarce Italian print. If this was indeed the case, it may be queried whether the title at least was not his—Joseph, according to the legend, having been the first missionary to Britain. The original, if original there was, certainly was not the work of Michael Angelo, to whom Blake chose to attribute it. Scarcely was he out of his articles than he produced (1779) two engravings from the history of England, *The Penance of Jane Shore* and *King Edward and Queen Eleanor*. These were after two water-colour drawings, selected from a much greater number with which he had amused the leisure hours of his apprenticeship. Mr. Gilchrist says that these and other works of the period have little of the peculiar Blakean quality, except the striking design *Morning, or Glad Day*, dated 1780, a facsimile of which is given here. This, indeed, is Blake all over, and would have made an excellent frontispiece for the poems with which he was about to herald the dawn of a new era in English poetry, though in all probability designed as an illustration of the lines in *Romeo and Juliet*;

> Night's candles are burnt out, and jocund day
> Stands tiptoe on the misty mountain tops.

A naked Apollo-like figure, wearing the dawn for a halo, in whom one fancifully traces a resemblance to Goethe, alights throbbing with joy and victory on the peak of a mountain, while the waning moon, as would seem, sets behind him, and a winged beetle scuds away.

The poems to which reference has been made had meanwhile been slowly accumulating; if the language of the advertisement which heralded their publication is to be taken literally, they were now complete. Before appearing as a poet, however, Blake had to undergo his probation as a lover. He became enamoured of a pretty girl variously called Polly or Clara Woods. She rejected him. He fell into a melancholy, and was sent to Richmond for change of air. There he lodged with a nursery gardener named Boucher. The daughter of the house, Catherine, had been frequently asked whom she would like to marry, and had always replied that she had not seen the man. Coming on the night of Blake's arrival into the room where he was sitting with the rest of the family, she grew faint from the presentiment that she beheld her destined husband. On subsequently hearing of his disappointment with Clara Woods, she told him that she pitied, and he told her that he loved. They were married on August 18, 1782, Blake having, it is said, proved their mutual constancy by refraining from seeing her for a year, while he was toiling to save enough to render their marriage not utterly imprudent. His first care afterwards was to teach her to read and write, to which he afterwards added enough of the pictorial art to enable her to colour his drawings. A more devoted wife never lived, though her devotion wore in the eyes of strangers an aspect of formality, and was always tinged with awe.

Poetical Sketches, 1783, were the first-fruits of Blake's genius, composed, as asserted in the advertisement prefixed by his friends, between 1768 and 1777.[1] They are the only examples of his literary work devoid of artistic illustration; we ought not, consequently, to spend much time upon them, yet they are the most memorable of his works, for they are nothing short of miraculous, and alone among his productions mark an era. For a hundred and thirty years English poetry had been mainly artificial, the product of conscious effort ranging down from the superb art of *Paradise Lost* to the prettinesses of Pope's imitators, but seldom or never wearing the aspect of a spontaneous growth. This young obscure engraver was the first to show that it was still possible to sing as the bird sings; he and no other was the morning star which announced the new day of English poetry. Had even the verses been of inferior quality, such inspiration would have sufficed for fame, but Blake is as exquisite as original, and warbles such nightingale

[1] If, however, the "Kitty" of "I love the jocund dance" is Catherine Boucher, this poem at least must be later than 1780, unless the name has been substituted for another, as has been known to happen.

Morning, or Glad Day. From an engraving by W. Blake.

notes as England had not heard since Andrew Marvell forsook song for satire. The songs of Dryden, indeed, have great merit, but how they savour of the study compared with the artless melody of a strain like this!

How sweet I roamed from field to field,
And tasted all the summer's pride,
Till I the Prince of Love beheld,
Who in the sunny beams did glide!

He showed me lilies for my hair,
And blushing roses for my brow;
He led me through his gardens fair,
Where all his golden pleasures grow.

With sweet May dews my wings were wet,
And Phœbus fired my vocal rage;
He caught me in his silken net,
And shut me in his golden cage.

He loves to sit and hear me sing,
Then, laughing, sports and plays with me;
Then stretches out my golden wing,
And mocks my loss of liberty.

This is such a song as Marlowe might have written, but for a delicate eighteenth-century suggestion in the style, whose aroma is not quite that of the Elizabethan era. It is none the less one of the pieces which none but Blake could have produced. The characteristics of his style, indeed, are much less apparent in this early volume than in his subsequent productions. They are most conspicuous in the *Mad Song*, but a more pleasing if less intense example is the following:

SONG.

Love and harmony combine,
And around our souls entwine,
While thy branches mix with mine
And our roots together join.

Joys upon our branches sit,
Chirping loud and singing sweet;
Like gentle streams beneath our feet
Innocence and virtue meet.

Thou the golden fruit dost bear,
I am clad in flowers fair;
Thy sweet boughs perfume the air,
And the turtle buildeth there.

> There she sits and feeds her young,
> Sweet I hear her mournful song;
> And thy lovely leaves among,
> There is Love: I hear his tongue.
>
> There his charm'd nest he doth lay,
> There he sleeps the night away,
> There he sports along the day,
> And doth among our branches play.

Not the least remarkable of the *Poetical Sketches* are "Samson" and other short pieces in blank verse. They are marvellously Tennysonian; if imitation there was, it obviously was not on Blake's part. Who would have hesitated to ascribe these lines, addressed to the Evening Star, to the Laureate?

> Let thy west wind sleep on
> The lake; speak silence with thy glimmering eye
> And wash the dusk with silver.

Even more marvellous than the sentiment is the metre, which cannot be judged by a short passage. Well might it be said, "Thou hast hid these things from the wise and prudent, and revealed them unto babes," when the secret of melodious blank verse, withheld since the Civil War from all the highly cultured and in many respects highly gifted bards of England, is disclosed on the sudden to this half-educated young man. It is exemplified on a larger scale by the accompanying fragments of an intended tragedy on *Edward the Third*, which proves two things: first, that Blake was destitute of all dramatic faculty; secondly, that, notwithstanding, few have so thoroughly assimilated Shakespeare. Shakespeare stands almost alone among great poets in having had hardly any direct imitators. Every one, of course, has profited by the study of his art; but those most deeply indebted to him in this respect have felt the least disposed to reproduce his style. The reason is evident. Other writers are partial, Shakespeare is universal; the model is too vast for study. A deliberate imitation of Shakespeare would assuredly be a failure: imitation is only practicable when it is not deliberate but unconscious, the effluence of a mind so saturated with Shakespeare that it can for the time only express itself in Shakespearian numbers, and think under Shakespearian forms. Blake must have been in such a situation when he attempted *Edward the Third*, the direct fruit of his roamings among the regal tombs in the Abbey with Shakespeare's historical plays in his hand. The drama is childish, but the feeling approaches Shakespeare as nearly as Keats's early poems approach Spenser. The imitation, being spontaneous and unsought, is never senile, but every line reveals a youth whose soul is with Shakespeare, though his body may be in Golden Square. Yet the reproduction of Shakespeare's manner is never so exact as to conceal the fact that the poet is writing in the eighteenth and not in the sixteenth century. The following passage may serve as an example both of the closeness of Blake's affinity with Shakespeare and of the *nuances* of difference that serve to vindicate his originality.

> Last night beneath
> The moon I walked abroad when all had pitched
> Their tents, and all were still.
> I heard a blooming youth singing a song
> He had composed, and at each pause he wiped
> His dropping eyes. The ditty was "If he
> Returned victorious he should wed a maiden
> Fairer than snow and rich as midsummer."
> Another wept, and wished health to his father.
> I chid them both, but gave them noble hopes.
> These are the minds that glory in the battle,
> And leap and dance to hear the trumpet sound.

This is beautiful description, sentiment and metre, but these beauties sum up the attractions of Blake's dramatic fragment. The dramatic element is wanting, there is no action. This deficiency runs through his whole work, pictorial as well as literary, and explains why one capable of such sublime conceptions was nevertheless incapable of taking rank with the Miltons and Michael Angelos. His productions are full of tremendous scenes, the strivings and agonies of colossal unearthly powers realised by his own mind with a vividness which proves the intensity of his conceptions. Yet he seldom impresses the beholder with any sentiment of awe or terror. The cause is not solely the fantastic character of these conceptions, for the effect is the same when he deals with mankind, and represents it in the most thrilling crises of which humanity is capable. His representation of the plague, for instance, engraved in Gilchrist's biography, excites strong interest and curiosity, but nothing of the shuddering dismay with which we should view such a scene in actual life, and which is so powerfully conveyed in such works as Géricault's *Wreck of the Medusa* and Poole's *Solomon Eagle.* The reason seems to be that Blake was not only a visionary but also a mystic, and that mysticism is hardly compatible with tragic passion. The visionary, as in the instances of Dante and Bunyan, may realise every detail of his ideal conceptions with the force of actual perception, but it is the very essence of the mystic's creed that things are not what they seem, and the man who knows himself to be depicting a hieroglyphic will never grasp his subject with the force of him who feels that he is dealing with a concrete reality. The Hindoos are a nation of mystics who regard existence as an illusion, and their art labours under the same defects as Blake's; their drama especially, with all the charm of lovely arabesque, makes nothing of the strongest situations, save when these are of the pathetic order. For although the mystic cannot be exciting, he can be tender: and while Blake's efforts at the delineation of frantic passion or overwhelming catastrophes usually (there are exceptions) leave us unmoved, nothing can be more pathetic than some of his delineations, such, for example, as the famous illustration to Blair, of an old man approaching the grave.

It seems almost strange that verses, as contrary to the spirit of the age that gave them birth as prophetic of the ideals of the age to come, should have found friends willing to defray their cost. If, however, it is true that Flaxman was among these friends, Blake had met with one congenial spirit. A clergyman named Matthews, incumbent of Percy Chapel, Charlotte Street, is mentioned as another patron, and as the writer of the well-meaning but too apologetic preface. Through him Blake seems to have become acquainted with Flaxman. To the few then able to appreciate the poems, they might well have seemed indicative of a great poetical career, for they are exactly the sweet, wild, untaught, prelusive music wherewith youth, as yet unschooled by criticism and unawakened to its really profound problems, is wont to essay its art. Why was it that Blake, though rivalling these early attempts in his *Songs of Innocence* and *Songs of Experience*, never progressed further; and in by far the greater part of his subsequent poetry went off altogether upon a wrong track, so far at least as concerned poetry? Partly, we think, because his mind was almost entirely deficient in the plastic element. He could reproduce a scene ready depicted for him, as in his illustrations to Job; he could embody a solitary thought with exquisite beauty, whether in poetry or in painting; but he could not combine his ideas into a whole. His faculty was purely lyrical, and when this evanescent endowment forsook him, devoid as he was of all plastic literary power, he had no Oenone or Ulysses to replace his Claribels and Eleanores. His verse became a mere accompaniment of his pictorial art, and harmonising with its vagueness and obscurity, necessarily lacked the symmetry with which a colourist can dispense, but which is essential to a poet. Even more remarkable than the music of Blake's early verses, unparalleled in their age, is the fact, vouched for by J. T. Smith, the biographer of Nollekens and Keeper of Prints at the British Museum, that he had composed tunes for them, which he could only repeat by ear from his ignorance of musical notation. Some of these, Smith says, were exquisitely beautiful.

At the appearance of the *Poetical Sketches* (1783), Blake had for a year been a married man, and was actively striving to make a living as an engraver. Most of his work of this nature at this time was executed after Stothard. It cannot be disputed that this graceful artist largely influenced Blake's style in its more idyllic aspects; whether, as he was afterwards inclined to assert, Stothard's invention owed something to him is not easy to determine. In 1784 he lost his father, a mild, pious man, who had well performed his duty to his son. Blake's elder brother James took his business, and the artist, who had probably inherited some little property, returned from Green Street to Broad Street, and, establishing himself next door to his brother, launched into speculation as a print-seller in partnership with a former fellow apprentice named Parker, taking his brother Robert as a gratuitous pupil. In 1785 he sent four drawings to the Academy. Three, illustrative of the story of Joseph, were shown in the International Exhibition of 1862, and are described by Gilchrist as "full of soft tranquil beauty, specimens of Blake's earlier style; a very different one from that of his later and better-known works." This is probably as much as to say that he then wrought much under the influence of Stothard, after whom he engraved the subject from *David Simple* given here; for the earlier design illustrative of the passage in *Romeo and Juliet* is characteristically Blakean. Mr. Gilchrist adds, "the design is correct and blameless, not to say tame (for Blake), the colour full, harmonious and sober." Mr. Rossetti says that the figure of Joseph, in the third drawing, "is especially pure and impulsive."

In 1787 Blake's experiment in print-selling came to an end, through disagreements, it is said, with his partner; but as neither appears to have

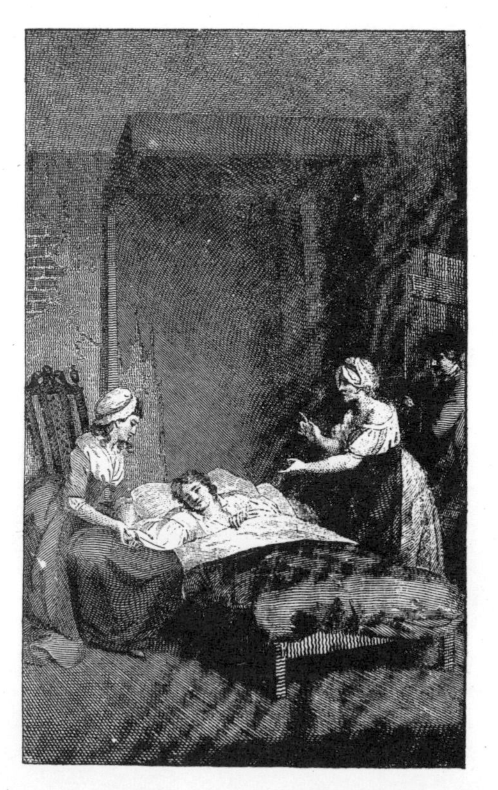

Illustration from "David Simple." Engraved by W. Blake after T. Stothard, R.A.

afterwards pursued the calling, it is probable that it had never been profitable. Parker obtained some distinction as an engraver, chiefly after Stothard, and died in 1805. In February, 1787, Blake had sustained a severe loss in the death of his brother and pupil Robert. Blake himself nursed the patient for some weeks, and when at last the end came, it is not surprising that he should have beheld his brother's spirit "arise and clap its hands for joy." Not long after, as he asserted, the spirit appeared to him in a dream, and revealed to him that process of printing from copper plates which, as we shall see, had the most decisive influence upon his work as an artist. Writing to Hayley in 1800, he says, "Thirteen years ago I lost a brother, and with his spirit I converse daily and hourly in the spirit, and see him in remembrance in the regions of my imagination. I hear his advice, and even now write from his dictate." "The ruins of Time," he finely subjoins, "build mansions in Eternity."

From this time Blake's sole assistant was his wife, whom he carefully instructed, and who tinted many of the coloured drawings which henceforth form the more characteristic portion of his work. After giving up his business as a print-seller, he removed from Broad Street to 28, Poland Street. Messrs. Ellis and Yeats conjecture that this may have been to escape the blighting influence of his commercial brother next door, but it is more probable that his venture had impoverished him, and that he was obliged to give up housekeeping.

CHAPTER II

Blake's Technical Methods—"Songs of Innocence" and "Songs of Experience"—Life in Poland Street and in Lambeth—Mystical Poetry and Art.

It was during his residence in Poland Street that Blake first appeared in that mingled character of poet and painter which marks him off so conspicuously from other painters and other poets. Painting has often been made the handmaid of poetry; it was Blake's idea, without infringing upon this relationship, to make poetry no less the handmaid of painting by employing his verse, engraved and beautified with colour, to enhance the artistic value of his designs, as well as to provide them with the needful basis of subject. The same principle may probably be recognised in those Oriental scrolls where the graceful labour of the scribe is as distinctly a work of art as the illustration of the miniaturist; but of these Blake can have known nothing. Necessity was with him the mother of invention. Since the appearance of *Poetical Sketches* he had written much that he desired to publish—but how to pay for printing? So severely had he suffered by his unfortunate commercial adventure that when at length, as he firmly believed, the new process by which his song and his design could be facsimiled together was revealed by his brother's spirit in a dream, a half-crown was the only coin his wife and he possessed between them in the world. One shilling and tenpence of this was laid out in providing the necessary materials.

The technical method to which Blake now resorted is thus described by Mr. Gilchrist: "It was quite an original one. It consisted of a species of engraving in relief, both words and designs. The verse was written and the designs and marginal embellishments outlined on the copper with an impervious liquid, probably the ordinary stopping-out varnish of engravers. Then all the white parts or lights, the remainder of the plate that is, were eaten away with aquafortis or other acid, so that the outline of letter and design was left prominent, as in stereotype. From these plates he printed off in any tint, yellow, brown, blue, required to be the prevailing or ground colour in his facsimiles; red he used for the letterpress. The page was then coloured up by hand in imitation of the original drawing with more or less variety of detail in the local hues. He ground and mixed his water-colours himself on a piece of statuary marble, after a method of his own, with common carpenter's glue diluted. The colours he used were few and simple: indigo, cobalt, gamboge, vermilion, Frankfort-black freely, ultramarine rarely, chrome not at all. These he applied with a camel's-hair brush, not with a sable, which he disliked. He taught Mrs. Blake to take off the impressions with care and delicacy, which such plates signally needed; and also to help in tinting them from his drawings with right artistic feeling; in all of which tasks she, to her honour, much delighted. The size of the plates was small, for the sake of economising copper, something under five inches by three. The number of engraved pages in the *Songs of Innocence* alone was twenty-seven. They were done up in boards by Mrs. Blake's hand, forming a small octavo; so that the poet and his wife did everything in making the book, writing, designing, printing, engraving,—everything except manufacturing the paper; the very ink, or colour rather, they did make. Never before, surely, was a man so literally the author of his own book."

The total effect of this process is tersely expressed by Mr. Rossetti, "The art is made to permeate the poetry." It resulted in the publication of *Songs of Innocence* in 1789, two years after its discovery or revelation. Other productions, of that weird and symbolic character in which Blake came more and more to delight, followed in quick succession. These will claim copious notice, but for the present we may pass on to *Songs of Experience*, produced in 1794, so much of a companion volume to *Songs of Innocence* that the two are usually found within the same cover. Neither attracted much attention at the time. Charles Lamb says: "I have heard of his poems, but have never seen them." He is, however, acquainted with "Tiger, tiger," which he pronounces "glorious." The price of the two sets when issued together was from thirty shillings to two guineas—an illustration of the material service which Art can render

From Blake's "Songs of Innocence."

From Blake's "Songs of Innocence."

to Poetry when it is considered that, published simply as poems, they would in that age have found no purchasers at eighteenpence. This price was nevertheless absurdly below their real value, and was enhanced even during the artist's lifetime. It came to be five guineas, and late in his life friends, from the munificent Sir Thomas Lawrence downwards, would commission sets tinted by himself at from ten to twenty guineas as a veiled charity.

Of the poems and illustrations in *Songs of Innocence* and *Songs of Experience* Gilchrist justly declares that their warp and woof are formed in one texture, and that to treat of them separately is like pulling up a daisy by the roots out of the green sward in which it springs. One essential characteristic inspires them both, and may be defined as childish fearlessness, the innocent courage of the infant who puts his hand upon the serpent and the cockatrice. Any one but Blake would have feared to publish designs and verses apparently so verging upon the trivial, and which indeed would have been trivial—and worse, affected—if the emanation of almost any other brain, or the execution of almost any other hand. Being his, their sincerity is beyond question, and they are a valuable psychological document as establishing the possibility of a man of genius and passion reaching thirty with the simplicity of a child. Hardly anything else in literature or art, unless some thought in Shakespeare, so powerfully conveys the impression of a pure elemental force, something absolutely spontaneous, innocent of all contact with and all influence from the refinements of culture. They certainly are not as a rule powerful, and contrast forcibly with the lurid and gigantic conceptions which if we did not remember that the same Dante depicted *The Tower of Famine* and *Matilda gathering Flowers*, we could scarcely believe to have proceeded from the same mind. Their impressiveness proceeds from a different source ; their primitive innocence and simplicity, and the rebuke which they seem to administer to artifice and refinement. Even great artists and inspired poets, suddenly confronted with such pure unassuming nature, may be supposed to feel as the disciples must have felt when the Master set the little child among them. No more characteristic examples could have been given than "The Lamb" and "Infant Joy" from *Songs of Innocence*, and "The Fly" and "The Tiger" from *Songs of Experience* selected for reproduction here from an uncoloured copy in the library of the British Museum. There is frequently a great difference in the colouring of the copies. That in the Museum Print Room is in full rich colour, while others are very lightly and delicately tinted.

It is of course much easier to convey an idea of the merits of Blake's

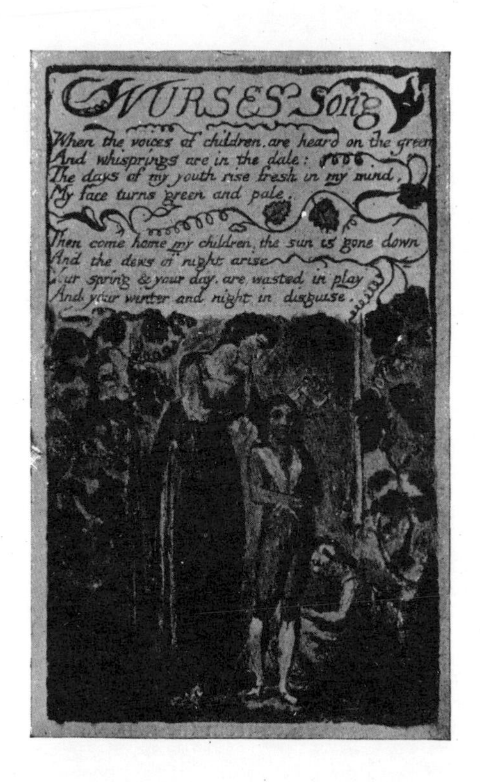

From a coloured copy of the "Songs of Innocence and Experience." British Museum.

verse than of his painting, for the former loses nothing by transcription, and the latter everything. The merit of the latter, too, is a variable quantity, depending much upon the execution of the coloured plates. The uncoloured are but phantoms of Blake's ideas. The general characteristics of his art in these books may be described as caressing tenderness and gentle grace, evinced in elegant human figures, frequently drooping like willows or recumbent like river deities, and in sinuous stems and delicate sprays, often as profuse as delicate. The foliated ornament in "On Another's Sorrow," for instance, seems like a living thing, and would almost speak without the aid of the accompanying verse. The figures usually are too small to impress by themselves, and rather seem subsidiary parts of the general design than the dominant factors. They mingle with the inanimate nature portrayed, as one note of a multitudinous concert blends with another. Yet "The Little Girl Found" tells its story by itself powerfully enough; and the innocent Bacchanalianism of the chorus in the "Laughing Song" is conveyed with truly Lyæan spirit and energy.

The prevalent cheerfulness of the *Songs of Innocence* is of course modified in *Songs of Experience*. The keynote of the former is admirably struck in the introductory poem:—

Piping down the valleys wild,
  Piping songs of pleasant glee,
On a cloud I saw a child,
  And he laughing said to me.

"Pipe a song about a Lamb!"
  So I piped with merry cheer.
"Piper, pipe that song again."
  So I piped; he wept to hear.

"Drop thy pipe, thy happy pipe;
  Sing thy songs of happy cheer!"
So I sang the same again.
  While he wept with joy to hear.

"Piper, sit thee down and write
  In a book, that all may read."
So he vanished from my sight;
  And I plucked a hollow reed.

And I made a rural pen,
  And I stained the water clear,
And I wrote my happy songs
  Every child may joy to hear.

This incarnate enigma among men could manifestly be as transparent as crystal when he knew exactly what he wished to say—a remark which may not be useless to the student of his mystical and prophetical writings. The character of *Songs of Experience*, published in 1794, when

Frontispiece of Mary Wollstonecraft's "Stories."

he had attained the age so cften fatal to men of genius, is conveyed more symbolically, yet intelligibly, in "The Angel":—

> I dreamt a dream! What can it mean?
> And that I was a maiden Queen
> Guarded by an Angel mild:
> Witless woe was ne'er beguiled!

THE FLY.

Little Fly
Thy summers play,
My thoughtless hand
Has brush'd away.

Am not I
A fly like thee?
Or art not thou
A man like me?

For I dance
And drink & sing:
Till some blind hand
Shall brush my wing.

If thought is life
And strength & breath:
And the want
Of thought is death;

Then am I
A happy fly,
If I live,
Or if I die.

From Blake's "Songs of Experience."

The Tyger.

Tyger Tyger, burning bright,
In the forests of the night;
What immortal hand or eye,
Could frame thy fearful symmetry?

In what distant deeps or skies.
Burnt the fire of thine eyes?
On what wings dare he aspire?
What the hand, dare sieze the fire?

And what shoulder, & what art,
Could twist the sinews of thy heart?
And when thy heart began to beat,
What dread hand? & what dread feet?

What the hammer? what the chain,
In what furnace was thy brain?
What the anvil? what dread grasp,
Dare its deadly terrors clasp?

When the stars threw down their spears
And water'd heaven with their tears:
Did he smile his work to see?
Did he who made the Lamb make thee?

Tyger Tyger burning bright,
In the forests of the night:
What immortal hand or eye,
Dare frame thy fearful symmetry?

From Blake's "Songs of Experience."

And I wept both night and day,
And he wiped my tears away;
And I wept both day and night,
And hid from him my heart's delight.

So he took his wings and fled;
Then the man blushed very red.
I dried my tears and armed my fears
With ten thousand shields and spears.

Soon my Angel came again;
I was armed, he came in vain;
For the time of youth was fled,
And gray hairs were on my head.

Generally speaking, the *Songs of Experience* may be said to answer to their title. They exhibit an awakening of thought and an occupation with metaphysical problems alien to the *Songs of Innocence.* Such a stanza as this shows that Blake's mind had been busy:—

Nought loves another as itself
  Nor venerates another so;
Nor is it possible to thought
  A greater than itself to know.

These ideas, however, are always conveyed, as in the remainder of the poem quoted, through the medium of a concrete fact represented by the poet. Perhaps the finest example of this fusion of imagination and thought is this stanza of the most striking and best known of all the poems, "The Tiger":—

When the stars threw down their spears
And watered heaven with their tears,
Did he smile his work to see?
Did He who made the lamb make thee?

An evident, though probably unconscious, reminiscence of "When the morning stars sang together, and all the sons of God shouted for joy," and like it for that extreme closeness to the inmost essence of things which the author of the Book of Job enjoyed in virtue of the primitive simplicity of his age and environment, and Blake through a childlike temperament little short of preternatural in an age like ours. It may be added, that although the pieces in *Songs of Innocence* and *Songs*

Page of Young's "Night Thoughts." Illustrated by W. Blake.

of Experience are of very unequal degrees of poetical merit, none want the infallible mark of inspired poetry—spontaneous, inimitable melody.

Both the simplicity and the melody, however, are absent from the remarkable works with which Blake had been occupying himself during the interval between the publication of the two series of his songs, which, with their successors, have given him a peculiar and unique reputation in their own weird way, but could not by themselves have given him the reputation of a poet. Blake's plain prose, as we shall see, is much more effective. In a strictly artistic point of view, nevertheless, these compositions reveal higher capacities than would have been inferred from the idyllic beauty of the pictorial accompaniments of *Songs of Innocence and Experience.* Before discussing these it will be convenient to relate the chief circumstances of Blake's life during the period of their production, and up to the remarkable episode of his migration to Felpham. They were not memorable or striking, but one of them had considerable influence upon his development. In 1791 he was employed by Johnson, the Liberal publisher of St. Paul's Churchyard, and as such a minor light of his time, to illustrate Mary Wollstonecraft's *Tales for Children* with six plates, both designed and engraved by him, one of which accompanies this essay. They are much in the manner of Stothard. This commission brought Blake as a guest to Johnson's house, where he became acquainted with a republican coterie—Mary Wollstonecraft, Godwin, Paine, Holcroft, Fuseli—with whose political opinions he harmonised well, though totally dissimilar in temperament from all of them, except Fuseli, who gave him several tokens of interest and friendship. These acquaintanceships, and the excitement of the times, led Blake to indite, and, which is more extraordinary, Johnson to publish, the first of an intended series of seven poetical books on the French Revolution. This, Gilchrist tells us, was a thin quarto, without illustrations, published without Blake's name, and priced at a shilling. Gilchrist probably derived this information from a catalogue, for he carefully avoids claiming to have seen the book, which seems to have also escaped the researches of all Blake's other biographers. It must be feared that it is entirely lost. Gilchrist must, however, have known something more of it if his assertion that the other six books were actually written but not printed, "events taking a different turn from the anticipated one," is based upon anything besides conjecture.

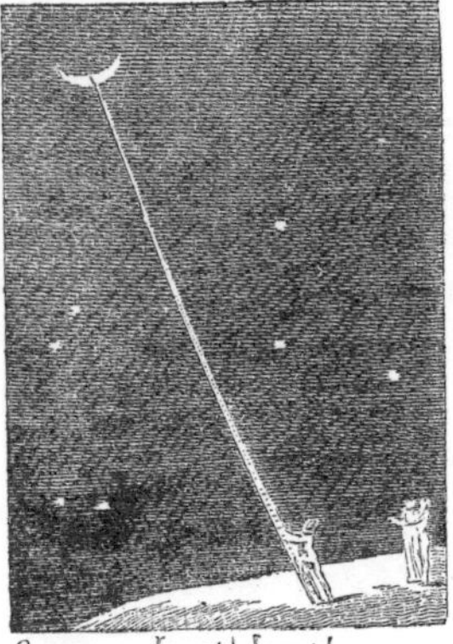

9 I want! I want!

10 Help! Help!

In 1793 Blake removed from Poland Street to Hercules Buildings, Lambeth, then a row of suburban cottages with little gardens. Here he

11 Aged Ignorance

15 Death's Door.

engraved his friend Flaxman's designs for the *Odyssey*, to replace plates engraved by Piroli and lost in the voyage from Italy, whence Flaxman had returned after seven years' absence. In 1795 he designed three illustrations for Stanley's translation of Burger's "Lenore," and in 1796 executed a much more important work, 537 drawings for an edition of Young's *Night Thoughts* projected by a publisher named Edwards. Forty-three were engraved and published in 1797, but the undertaking was carried no further for want of encouragement, and the designs, after remaining long in the publisher's family, eventually came into the hands of Mr. Bain of the Haymarket, who is still the possessor. The most important are described by Mr. Frederic Shields in the appendix to the second volume of Gilchrist's biography. Mr. Shields' descriptions are so fascinating[1] that from them alone one would be inclined to rate the drawings very high : but Mr. Gilchrist thinks these ill adapted for the special purpose of book illustration which they were destined to subserve, and reminds us that the absence of colour is a grave loss. Blake is said to have been paid only a guinea a plate for the forty-three engravings, on which he worked for a year. The Lambeth period, however, seems not to have been an unprosperous one, for he had many pupils. Several curious anecdotes of it were related after his death on the alleged authority of Mrs. Blake, but their truth seems doubtful. It is certain that during this period he met with the most constant of his patrons, Mr. Thomas Butts, who for nearly thirty years continued a steady buyer of his drawings, and but for whom he would probably have fallen into absolute distress.

It is now time to speak of the literary works—"pictured poesy," like the woven poesy of *The Witch of Atlas*—produced during this period. In 1789, the year of publication of the *Songs of Innocence*, the series opens with *Thel.* In 1790 comes *The Marriage of Heaven and Hell* ; in 1793, *The Gates of Paradise*, *The Vision of the Daughters of Albion*, and *America* ; in 1794, *Europe, A Prophecy*, and *Urizen* ; in 1795, *The Song of Los*, and *The Book of Ahaniah.* In 1797 Blake seems to have written, or to have begun to write, the mystical poem ultimately entitled *Vala*, never published by him, and more than fifty years after his death found

[1] As for example "Man lies by a rock-bound shore, his thoughts flying forth from him in likeness of delicate airy figures driven by the wind to perish in the endless sea as soon as born." In the absence of the drawings themselves such descriptions affect us like the projects for unwritten stories in Hawthorne's *American Note Book*.

in Linnell's possession in such a state of confusion that it took Messrs. Ellis and Yeats days to arrange the MS., which they fondly deem to be now in proper order. It is printed in the third volume of their work on Blake. *Tiriel* is undated, but would seem to be nearly contemporary with *Thel.*

The Gates of Paradise constitutes an exception to the general spirit of the works of this period, the accompanying text, though mystical enough, being lyrical and not epical. The seventeen beautiful designs, emblematical of the incidents necessarily associated with human nature, are well described by Allan Cunningham as "a sort of devout dream, equally wild and lovely."

The merits of this remarkable series of works will always be a matter of controversy. "Whether," as Blake himself says, "whether this is Jerusalem or Babylon, we know not." It must be so, for they are purely subjective, there is no objective criterion; they admit of comparison with nothing, and can be tested by no recognised rules. In the whole compass of human creation there is perhaps hardly anything so distinctively an emanation of the mind that gave it birth. Visions they undoubtedly are, and, as Messrs. Ellis and Yeats well say, they are manifestly not the production of a pretender to visionary powers. Whatever Blake has here put down, pictorially or poetically, is evidently a record of something actually discerned by the inner eye. This, however, leaves the question of their value still open. To the pictorial part, indeed, almost all are agreed in attaching a certain value, though the warmth of appreciation is widely graduated. But literary estimation is not only discrepant but hostile; some deem them revelation, others rhapsody. The one thing certain is the general tendency towards Pantheism which Mr. Swinburne has made the theme of an elaborate essay. To us they seem an exemplification of the truth that no man can serve two masters. Blake had great gifts, both as poet and artist, and he aspired not only to employ both, but to combine both in the same work. At first this was practicable, but soon the artistic faculty grew while the poetical dwindled. Not only did the visible speech of painting become more important to him than the viewless accents of verse, but his poetry became infected with the artistic method. He allowed a latitude to his language which he ought to have reserved for his form and colour, and became as hieroglyphic in a speech where hieroglyphs are illegitimate as in one where they are permissible. This is proved by the fact that the decline in the purity of poetical form and in the perspicuity of poetical language proceed *pari passu*. *Thel*, the earliest, is also both the most luminous and the most musical of these pieces. Could Blake have schooled himself to have written such blank verse as he had already produced in *Edward the Third* and *Samson*, *Thel* would have been a very fine poem. Even as it is its lax, rambling semi-prose is full of delicate modulations :

> The daughters of the Seraphim led round their sunny flocks,
> All but the youngest ; she in paleness sought the secret air
> To fade away like morning beauty from her mortal day.
> Down by the river of Adera her soft voice is heard,
> And thus her gentle lamentation falls like morning dew.

In every succeeding production, however, there is less of metrical beauty, and thought and expression grow continually more and more amorphous. Blake may not improbably have been influenced by Ossian, whose supposed poems were popular in his day, and from whom some of his proper names, such as Usthona, seem to have been adopted. Many then deemed that Ossian had demonstrated form to be a mere accident o poetry instead of, as in truth it is, an indissoluble portion of its essence. There is certainly a strong family resemblance between Blake's shadowy conceptions and Ossian's misty sublimities. On the other hand, h may be credited with having made a distinguished disciple in Wal Whitman, who would not, we think, have written as he did if Blak had never existed. What was pardonable in one so utterly devoi of the sentiment of beautiful form as Whitman, was less so in one s exquisitely gifted as Blake. Both derive some advantages from thei laxity, especially the poet of Democracy, but both suffer from the inabilit of poetry, divorced from metrical form, to take a serious hold upon th memory. One reads and admires, and by and by the sensation is of th passage of a great procession of horsemen and footmen and banners, bu no distinct impression of a single countenance.

The general effect of these strange works upon the average min is correctly expressed by Gilchrist, when he says, speaking of *Europe* : "I is hard to trace out any distinct subject, any plan or purpose, or to deter mine whether it mainly relates to the past, the present, or things to con

And yet its incoherence has a grandeur about it as of the utterance of a man whose eyes are fixed on strange and awful sights, invisible to bystanders." What, then, did Blake suppose himself to behold? Messrs. Ellis and Yeats have devoted an entire volume of their three-volume work on Blake to the exposition of his visions. Their comment is often highly suggestive, but it is seldom convincing. When the right interpretation of a symbol has been found, it is usually self-evident. Not so with their explanations, which appear neither demonstrably wrong nor demonstrably right. Not that Blake talked aimless nonsense; we are conscious of a general drift of thought in some particular direction which seems to us to offer a general affinity to the thought of the ancient Gnostics. It would be interesting if some competent person would endeavour to determine whether the resemblance goes any deeper than externals. Blake certainly knew nothing of the Gnostics at first hand, nor is it probable that he could have gained any knowledge of them from the mystical writers he did study, Behmen and Swedenborg. But similar tendencies will frequently incarnate themselves in individuals at widely remote periods of the world's history without evidence of direct filiation. Even so exceptional a personage as Blake cannot be considered apart from his age, and his age, among its other aspects, was one of mesmerism and illuminism. The superficial resemblance of his writings to those of the Gnostics is certainly remarkable. Both embody their imaginations in concrete forms; both construct elaborate cosmogonies and obscure myths; both create hierarchies of principalities and powers, and equip their spiritual potentates with sonorous appellations; both disparage matter and its Demiurgus. "I fear," said Blake to Robinson, "that Wordsworth loves nature, and nature is the work of the devil. The devil is in us as far as we are nature." The chief visible difference, that the Gnostics' philosophy tends to asceticism, and Blake's to enjoyment, may perhaps be explained by the consideration that he was a poet, and that they were philosophers and divines. Perhaps the best preparation for any student of Blake who might wish to investigate this subject further would be to read the article in the *Dictionary of Christian Biography* upon the *Pistis Sophia*, the only Gnostic book that has come down to us, and one which Blake would have delighted in illustrating. The Gnostic belief in the all-importance of the

TITLE PAGE FROM THE BOOK OF THEL.

transcendent knowledge which comes of immediate perception (γνῶσις) reappears in him with singular intensity. "Men are admitted into heaven," he says, "not because they have curbed and governed their passions, or have no passions, but because they have cultivated their understandings. The fool shall not enter into heaven, let him be ever so holy." Nothing in Blake, perhaps, is so Gnostic as the strange poem, *The Everlasting Gospel*, first published by Mr. Rossetti, though many things in it would have shocked the Gnostics.

The strictly literary criticism of Blake's mystical books may be almost confined to the *Book of Thel*, for this alone possesses sufficient symmetry to allow a judgment to be formed upon it as a whole. The others are like quagmires occasionally gay with brilliant flowers; but *Thel*, though its purpose may be obscure, is at all events coherent, with a beginning and an end. Thel, "youngest daughter of the Seraphim," roves through the lower world lamenting the mortality of beautiful things, including her own. All things with which she discourses offer her consolation, but to no purpose. At last she enters the realm of Death himself.

> The eternal gates' terrific porter lifted the northern bar;
> Thel entered in and saw the secrets of the land unknown.
> She saw the couches of the dead, and where the fibrous root
> Of every heart on earth infixes deep its restless twists:
> A land of sorrows and of tears, where never a smile was seen.
>
> She wandered in the land of clouds, through valleys dark listening
> Dolours and lamentations; waiting oft beside a dewy grave
> She stood in silence, listening to the voices of the ground,
> Till to her own grave-plot she came, and there she sat down,
> And heard this voice of sorrow breathed from the hollow pit.

The effect of the voice of sorrow upon Thel is answerable to that of the spider upon little Miss Muffet. This abrupt conclusion injures the effect of a piece which otherwise may be compared to a strain of soothing music, suggestive of many things, but giving definite expression to none. Messrs. Ellis and Yeats, however, have no difficulty in assigning a meaning. Thel, according to them, is "the pure spiritual essence," her grief is the dread of incarnation, and her ultimate flight is a return "to the land of pure unembodied innocence from whence she came." Yet her forsaking this land is represented as her own act, and it is difficult to see how she could have "led round her sunny flocks" in it if she had not been embodied while she inhabited it. At the same time, if Messrs. Ellis and Yeats are right, no interpretation of Blake can be disproved by any inconsistency that it may seem to involve. "The surface," they say, "is perpetually, as it were, giving way before one, and revealing another surface below it, and that again dissolves when we try to

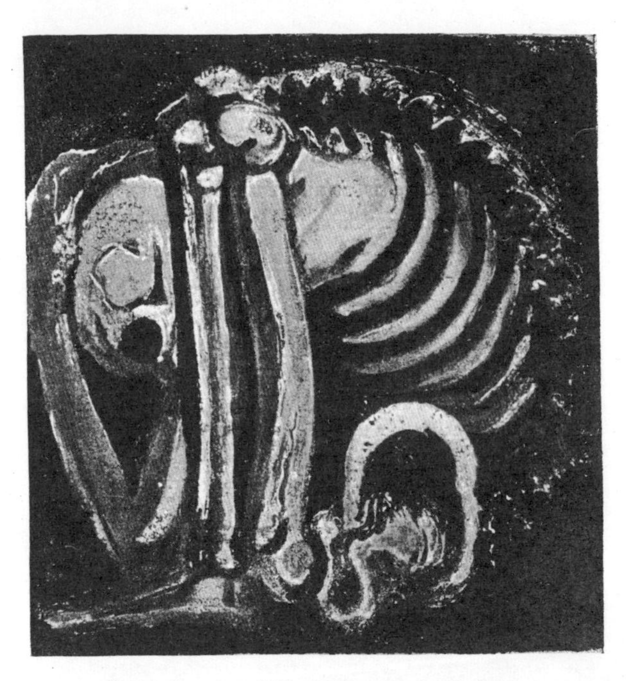

Design from the "Book of Urizen." By W. Blake.

study it. The making of religions melts into the making of the earth, and that fades away into some allegory of the rising and the setting of the sun. It is all like a great cloud full of stars and shapes, through which the eye seeks a boundary in vain."

Mr. Yeats, putting his interpretation of Blake's symbolism more tersely into the preface to his excellent edition of the Poetical Works, describes it as shadowing forth the endless conflict between the Imagination and the Reason, which, we may add, the Gnostics would have expressed as the strife between the Supreme Deity and the god of this world, the very phrase which Mr. Yeats himself uses in describing Urizen, Blake's Evil Genius, "the maker of dead law and blind negation," contrasted as the Gnostics would have contrasted him with Los, the deity of the living world. Blake, therefore, has points of contact with the representatives of the French Revolution on one side, and with Coleridge on the other. Mr. Yeats's interpretation is in itself coherent and plausible, but the question whether it can be fairly deduced from Blake himself is one on which few are entitled to pronounce, and the causes of Blake's obscurity are not so visible as its consequences. To us, as already said, much of it appears to arise from his imperfect discrimination between the provinces of speech and of painting. His discourse frequently seems a hieroglyphic which would have been more intelligible if it could have been expressed in the manner proper to hieroglyphics by pictorial representation. As Mr. Smetham says of some of the designs, "Thought cannot fathom the secret of their power, and yet the power is there." It seems evident that the poem, when a complete lyric, generally preceded the picture in Blake's mind, and that the latter must usually be taken as a gloss, in which he seeks to illustrate by means of visible representation what he was conscious of having left obscure by verbal expression. The exquisite song of the Sunflower, for example, certainly existed before the very slight accompanying illustration.

> Ah Sunflower, weary of time,
> Who counted the steps of the sun,
> Seeking after that sweet golden clime
> Where the traveller's journey is done.
>
> Where the youth, pined away with desire,
> And the pale virgin shrouded in snow,
> Arise from their graves and aspire
> Where my sunflower wishes to go.

The first of these stanzas is perfectly clear : the second requires no interpretation to a poetical mind, but will not bear construing strictly, and its comprehension is certainly assisted by the slight fugitive design lightly traced around the border. Generally the pictorial illustration of Blake's thought is much more elaborate, but in *Songs of Innocence and*

Experience it almost always seems to have grown out of the poem. In the less inspired *Prophetical Books*, on the other hand, the pictorial representation, even when present only to the artist's mind, seems to have frequently suggested or modified the text. An example may be adduced from *The Book of Thel.*

> Why an ear, a whirlpool fierce to draw creations in?

Blake had noted the external likeness of the convolutions of the ear to the convolutions of a whirlpool; therefore the ear shall be described as actually being what it superficially resembles, and because the whirlpool sucks in ships, the ear shall suck in creations. It must also be remembered that Blake's belief that his works were given him by inspiration prevented his revising them, and that they were stereotyped by the method of their publication. No considerable productions of the human mind, it is probable, so nearly approach the character of absolutely extemporaneous utterances.

Before passing from the literary to the artistic expression of Blake's genius in these books, something must be said of the remarkable appendix to *The Marriage of Heaven and Hell* entitled *Proverbs of Hell.* These are a number of aphoristic sayings, impregnated with Blake's peculiarities of thought and expression, but for the most part so shrewd and pithy as to demonstrate the author's sanity, at least at this time of his life. The following are some of the more striking:—

> Drive your cart and your plough over the bones of the dead.
> The road of excess leads to the palace of wisdom.
> A fool sees not the same tree that a wise man sees.
> All wholesome food is caught without a net or a trap.
> If the fool would persist in his folly he would become wise.
> The fox condemns the trap, not himself.
> The eagle never lost so much time as when he submitted to learn of the crow
> The fox provides for himself, but God provides for the lion.
> He who has suffered you to impose on him, knows you.
> The tigers of wrath are wiser than the horses of instruction.
> One law for the lion and ox is oppression.
> The best wine is the oldest, the best water the newest.

These are not the scintillations of reason which may occasionally illumine the chaos of a madman's brain, but bespeak a core of good

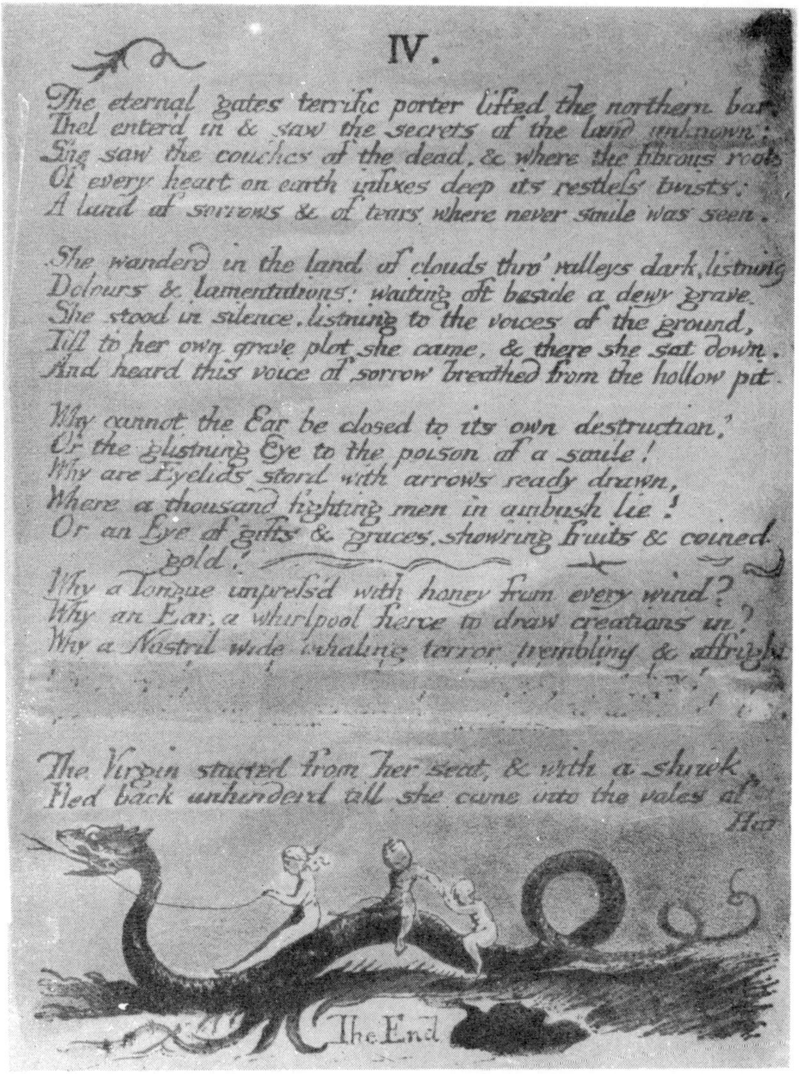

IV.

The eternal gates terrific porter lifted the northern bar:
Thel enterd in & saw the secrets of the land unknown;
She saw the couches of the dead, & where the fibrous roots
Of every heart on earth infixes deep its restless twists:
A land of sorrows & of tears where never smile was seen.

She wanderd in the land of clouds thro' valleys dark, listning
Dolours & lamentations: waiting oft beside a dewy grave
She stood in silence, listning to the voices of the ground,
Till to her own grave plot she came, & there she sat down.
And heard this voice of sorrow breathed from the hollow pit.

Why cannot the Ear be closed to its own destruction?
Or the glistning Eye to the poison of a smile!
Why are Eyelids stord with arrows ready drawn,
Where a thousand fighting men in ambush lie!
Or an Eye of gifts & graces, showring fruits & coined gold!
Why a Tongue impress'd with honey from every wind?
Why an Ear, a whirlpool fierce to draw creations in?
Why a Nostril wide inhaling terror trembling & affright.

The Virgin started from her seat, & with a shriek,
Fled back unhinderd till she came into the vales of Har

The End

FINAL PAGE FROM THE BOOK OF THEL.

sense quite inconsistent with general mental disturbance, though sufficiently compatible with delusion on particular subjects. With incomparable art, Shakespeare has imparted a touch of wildness to Hamlet's shrewdest sayings ; but Blake speaks rather as Polonius would have spoken if it had been possible for Polonius to speak in tropes.

From the difficult subject of the interpretation of Blake's mystical designs we pass with satisfaction to the artistic qualities of the designs themselves. On this point there is an approximation to unanimity. To some the sublime, to others the grotesque, may seem to preponderate, but all will allow them to be among the most remarkable and original series of conceptions that ever emanated from a mortal brain. To whatever exceptions they may be liable, it enlarges one's apprehension of the compass of human faculties to know that human faculties have been adequate to their production. They may be ranked with the most imaginative passages of *Paradise Lost*, and of Byron's *Cain* as an endeavour of the mind to project itself beyond the visible and tangible, and to create for itself new worlds of grandeur and of gloom in height and abyss and interstellar space. Wonderful indeed is the range of imagination displayed, even though we cannot shut our eyes to some palpable repetitions. In the opinion, however, of even so sympathetic a critic as Dr. Wilkinson, Blake deserves censure for having degenerated into mere monstrosity. "Of the worst aspect of Blake's genius," he says, "it is painful to speak. In his *Prophecies of America*, his *Visions of the Daughters of Albion*, and a host of unpublished drawings, earth-born might has banished the heavenlier elements of art, and exists combined with all that is monstrous and diabolical. The effect of these delineations is greatly heightened by the antiquity which is engraven on the faces of those who do and suffer in them. We have the impression that we are looking down into the hells of the ancient people, the Anakim, the Nephilim, and the Rephaim. Their human forms are gigantic petrifactions, from which the fires of lust and intense selfish passion have long dissipated what was animal and vital, leaving stony limbs and countenances expressive of despair and stupid cruelty." We, on the other hand, should rather criticise Blake for having failed to be as appalling as he meant to be. His power, as it seems to us, consisted rather in the vivid imagination than in the actual rendering of scenes of awe and horror. Far inferior artists have produced more thrilling effects of this sort with much simpler means. It would be wrong to say that his visions appear unreal, but they do appear at a remove from reality, a world seen through a glass darkly, its phantasm rather than its portrait. This, however, only applies to the inventions of Blake's own brain, which, if we may judge by the moderate development of the back head in Deville's cast, lacked the force of the animal propensities requisite for the portrayal of cruelty and horror. He could render the conceptions of others with startling force—witness the impressive delineation reproduced by us of the Architect of the Universe at work with his compasses ; and the simple pencil outline of Nebuchadnezzar in Mr. Rossetti's book, engraved by Gilchrist, where the human quadruped creeps away with an expression of overwhelming and horror-stricken dismay. This power of interpretation was to find yet finer expression in the illustration of the Book of Job.

Blake's technical defects are indicated by Messrs. Ellis and Yeats as consisting mainly in imperfect treatment of the human form from want of anatomical knowledge. He had always disliked that close study of the life which alone could have made him an able draughtsman ; it "obliterated" him, he said, and had resolved to quarrel with almost all the artists from whom he might have learned. It must be remembered in his excuse that consummate colouring and consummate draughtsmanship are seldom found associated. Those who may feel disappointed with the reproductions of Blake's mystical designs must also remember that these are but shadows of the artist's thought, which needed for its full effect the application of colour by his own hand. "Much," says Dante Rossetti, "which seems unaccountably rugged and incomplete is softened by the sweet, liquid, rainbow tints of the coloured copies into mysterious brilliancy." The effect thus obtained may perhaps be best shown by Mr. Gilchrist's eloquent description of the illuminated drawings in Lord Crewe's copy of *America.* "Turning over the leaves, it is sometimes like an increase of daylight in the retina, so fair and open is the effect of particular pages. The skies of sapphire, or gold, rayed with hues of sunset, against which stand out leaf or blossom, or pendent branch, gay with bright-plumaged birds ; the strips of emerald sward below, gemmed with flower and lizard, and enamelled

The Ancient of Days setting a Compass to the Earth. From a water-colour drawing by W. Blake. British Museum.

snake, refresh the eye continually. Some of the illustrations are of a more sombre kind. There is one in which a little corpse, white as snow, lies gleaming on the floor of a green over-arching cave, which close inspection proves to be a field of wheat, whose slender interlacing stalks, bowed by the full ear and by a gentle breeze, bend over the dead infant. The delicate network of stalks, which is carried up one side of the page, the main picture being at the bottom, and the subdued yet vivid green light shed over the whole, produce a lovely decorative effect. Decorative effect is, in fact, never lost sight of, even where the motive of the design is ghastly or terrible." Whatever the imperfections of Blake's peculiar sphere, it *was* his sphere, and probably the only department of art in which he could have obtained greatness even if his technical accomplishment had been as complete as it was the reverse. When painting on more orthodox lines he is often surprisingly tame and conventional. How remote he was from the inane when he could revel in his own conceptions may, notwithstanding the tremendous disadvantages inherent in reproduction, be judged from the illustrations to his mystical books selected for this monograph, the frontispiece and Plate IV. of *Thel*, and the two subjects from *America*.

CHAPTER III

Blake's removal to Felpham—Intercourse with Hayley—Return to London—"Jerusalem"—Connection with Cromek—Illustrations of Blair's "Grave"—Illustration of Chaucer's "Canterbury Pilgrims"—Exhibition of his Works and "Descriptive Catalogue."

BLAKE was now about to make a change in his external environment, which would have been momentous to any artist whose themes had been less exclusively discerned by the inner eye. It is an extraordinary fact, but there is absolutely no evidence that the poet who "made a rural pen" had as yet ever seen the country beyond the immediate neighbourhood of London. It is vain to speculate upon the precise modification which might have been wrought in his genius by rural nurture or foreign travel. Now he was actually to become a denizen of the country for some years. An introduction from Flaxman had made him acquainted with William Hayley, a Sussex squire and scholar, now chiefly remembered as his patron and the biographer of Cowper, but esteemed in his own day as one of the best representatives of English poetry at what seemed the period of its deepest decrepitude, though he is unaccountably omitted in Porson's catalogue of the bards of the epoch.[1] Hayley, having lost his son, a pupil of Flaxman, and his friend Cowper within a week of each other in the spring of 1800, resolved to solace his grief by writing Cowper's life, and suggested that Blake should live near him during the progress of the work to execute the engravings by which it was to be illustrated. In August, 1800, Blake removed from Lambeth to Felpham, near Bognor, on the Sussex coast, where Hayley occupied a marine villa, his own residence at Eastham being let on account of

[1] Poetis nos laetamur tribus,
Pye, Petro Pindar, parvo Pybus;
Si ulterius ire pergis,
Adde his Sir James Bland Burges.

the embarrassment of his affairs. The cottage was not provided by him for Blake, but the rent was paid by Blake himself. The change from Lambeth to a beautiful country of groves, meadows, and cornfields, with sails in the distance,

> Half lost in the liquid azure bloom of a crescent of sea,
> The shining sapphire-spangled marriage ring of the land,

affected Blake with enthusiastic delight. "Felpham," he wrote to Flaxman, "is a sweet place for study, because it is more spiritual than London. Heaven opens here on all sides her golden gates; her windows are not obstructed by vapours; voices of celestial inhabitants are more distinctly heard, and their forms more distinctly seen, and my cottage is also a shadow of their houses." He continues: "I am more famed in Heaven for my works than I could well conceive. In my brain are studies and chambers with books and pictures of old, which I wrote and painted in ages of eternity before my mortal life; and those works are the delight and study of archangels. Why then should I be anxious about the riches or fame of mortality?" It is clear that, notwithstanding his theories of the deadness of the material creation, Blake valued natural beauty as an instrument for bringing him into more intimate connection with the visionary world. At first the desired effect was fully produced. Blake began to compose, or rather, according to his own account, to take down from supernatural dictation the *Jerusalem*, the most important in some respects of his mystical writings. Walking by the shore—the very shore where Cary was afterwards to encounter Coleridge—he habitually met Moses and the Prophets, Homer, Dante, and Milton. "All," he said, "majestic shadows, gray but luminous, and superior to the common height." A description so fine, that some may be inclined to deem it something more than a mere fancy. Unfortunately he also fell in with a fairies' funeral, a stumbling-block to the most resolute faith. By and by, however, the dampness of the cottage proved provocative of rheumatism, and, which was much more disastrous, the mental climate proved unsympathetic. Hayley's patronage of so strange a creature as he must have thought Blake does him the highest honour. He appears throughout, not only as a very kind man, but, what is less usual in a literary per-

Fiery the Angels rose, & as they rose deep thunder roll'd
Around their shores: indignant burning with the fires of Orc
And Bostons Angel cried aloud as they flew thro' the dark
night.

He cried: Why trembles honesty and like a murderer,
Why seeks he refuge from the frowns of his immortal station,
Must the generous tremble & leave his joy, to the idle: to
the pestilence!
That mock him? who commanded this? what God? what Angel!
To keep the genrous from experience till the ungenerous
Are unrestraind performers of the energies of nature;
Till pity is become a trade, and generosity a science,
That men get rich by, & the sandy desart is giv'n to the strong
What God is he, writes laws of peace, & clothes him in a tempest
What pitying Angel lusts for tears, and fans himself with sighs
What crawling villain preaches abstinence & wraps himself
In fat of lambs? no more I follow, no more obedience pay.

From Blake's "America."

sonage, a very patient one. He actually instructed Blake in Greek. His kindness and patience did not, however, render him any the better poet; he was an elegant *dilettante* at the best, and Blake must have chafed at the obligation under which he felt himself to illustrate his verses. One ballad of some merit, however, "Little Tom the Sailor," inspired Blake with a striking if somewhat rude design, and he adorned Hayley's library with ideal portraits of illustrious authors. The engraving work which he had to execute for Hayley's life of Cowper was also little to his taste, but there seems no valid reason to charge him with neglect of it. His own self-reproach, indeed, ran in quite a different channel: he accused himself most seriously of unfaithfulness to his high vocation as a revealer and interpreter of spiritual things. Absence from town led him to write frequently to his friend and patron Butts, and these letters are invaluable indications not only of the frame of his mind at the time, but of its general habit. "I labour," he says, "incessantly, I accomplish not one-half of what I intend, because my abstract folly hurries me often away while I am at work, carrying me over mountains and valleys, which are not real, into a land of abstraction where spectres of the dead wander. This I endeavour to prevent; I, with my whole might, chain my feet to the world of duty and reality. But in vain! the faster I bind, the lighter is the ballast; for I, so far from being bound down, take the world with me in my flights, and often it seems lighter than a ball of wool rolled by the wind. . . . . If we fear to do the dictates of our angels, and tremble at the tasks set before us, if we refuse to do spiritual acts because of natural fears or natural desires, who can describe the dismal torments of such a state? . . . . Though I have been very unhappy, I am so no longer. I have travelled through perils and darkness not unlike a champion. I have conquered and shall go on conquering. Nothing can withstand the fury of my course among the stars of God and in the abysses of the accuser." In plain English Hayley strongly advised Blake to give up his mystical poetry and design and devote himself solely to engraving, and Blake looked upon the advice as a suggestion of the adversary. We do not know what Hayley said. If he thought that one of the *Poetical Sketches* or the *Songs of Innocence* was worth many pages of *Urizen* apart from the illustrations, he had reason for what he thought. But Blake's lyrical gift had all but forsaken him ; he was incapable of emitting "wood-notes wild," and the only way in which he could give literary expression to the inspiration by which he justly deemed himself visited was through his rhythmical form, which to Hayley may well have seemed monstrous. It is highly probable that the pictorial part of Blake's work found no more favour with Hayley than the poetical ; at all events it is very certain that he greatly preferred his engraving, and wished Blake to follow the art by which he had the best prospect of providing for himself. Johnson and Fuseli, by Blake's own admission, had given the same advice ; and an obscure line in one of his rather undignified and splenetic epigrams against his well-intentioned friend may be interpreted as meaning that Hayley had tried to bring his wife's influence to bear upon him for this end. In any case he lost temper with Hayley, and wrote to Butts (July, 1803) : "Mr. Hayley approves of my designs as little as he does of my poems, and I have been forced to insist on his leaving me in both to my own self-will ; for I am determined to be no longer pestered with his genteel ignorance and polite disapprobation. I know myself both poet and painter, and it is not his affected contempt that can move to anything but a more assiduous pursuit of both arts." Two months afterwards he returned to London, but on better terms with Hayley ; partly on account of the latter's generous conduct in providing for his defence against a charge of using seditious language, trumped up against him by a soldier whom he had turned out of his garden. "Perhaps," he wrote to Butts, "this was suffered to give opportunity to those whom I doubted to clear themselves of all imputation." The case was tried in January, 1804, and terminated in Blake's triumphant acquittal. An old man who had attended the trial as a youth said that he remembered nothing of it except Blake's flashing eye.

The engravings executed by Blake for Hayley during his residence at Felpham were six for the life and letters of Cowper ; four original designs for ballads by Hayley, including "Poor Tom," and six engravings after Maria T. Flaxman for Hayley's *Triumphs of Temper*. He did some work for Hayley after his return to town—engravings for the *Life of Romney*, and original designs for Hayley's *Ballads on Animals*—and corresponded with him in a friendly spirit, but the intimacy gradually died away.

Blake was profoundly influenced by his residence at Felpham in one respect ; he became acquainted with opposition, and distinctly realised a power antagonistic to his aspirations. He was thus stung into self-assertion, and became hostile to the artists whose aims and methods he was unable to reconcile with his ideas. The first hints of this attitude appear in the praises he bestows upon the work of his own which chiefly occupied him at Felpham, the *Jerusalem.* "I may praise it," he says, "since I dare not pretend to be any other than the secretary ; the authors are in eternity. I consider it as the grandest poem that this world contains. Allegory addressed to the intellectual powers, while it is altogether hidden from the corporeal understanding, is my definition of the most sublime poetry." Blake's allegory so effectually eludes both the reason and the understanding that Messrs. Ellis and Yeats frankly tell us that it is not for a moment to be supposed that their own elaborate interpretation will convey any idea to the mind unless it is read conjointly with the poem ; and if such is the commentary what must the text be ? If they are right the confusion is greatly increased by a wrong arrangement, and by the numerous interpolations which Blake subsequently introduced into the poem, which, though nominally issued in 1804, was not, they think, actually completed until about 1820. It suffers from being nearer prose than any of his former books "When this verse was dictated to me," he says, "I considered a monotonous cadence, like that used by Milton, Shakespeare, and all writers of English blank verse, derived from the modern bondage of rhyming, to be a necessary and indispensable part of the verse. But I soon found that in the mouth of a true orator such monotony was not only awkward, but as much a bondage as rhyme itself." What can be said of the ears that could find Shakespeare's and Milton's blank verse monotonous ? The truth is that Blake's originally exquisite perception of harmony had waned with his lyrical faculty, and he scoffs at what he is no longer able to produce. Yet the general grandiose effect of *Jerusalem* is undeniable. Little as we can attach any definite idea to it, it simultaneously awes and soothes like one of the great inarticulate voices of nature, the booming of the billows, or the whisper of the winds in the wood. Occasionally we encounter some beautiful little vignette like this :—

> She creates at her will a little moving night and silence,
> With spaces of sweet gardens and a tent of elegant beauty,
> Closed in by sandy deserts, and a night of stars shining ;
> A little tender moon, and hovering angels on the wing,
> And the male gives a time and revolution to her space
> Till the time of love is passed in ever-varying delights :
> For all things exist in the human imagination.

This seems an illustration of what we have said of the dependence of Blake's poetry upon his pictorial imagination, for it is clearly nothing but a magnificent expansion of the midsummer night idyl of the glowworm shining for her mate, "with her little drop of moonlight," as Beddoes beautifully says.

In artistic merit *Jerusalem* is fully equal to any of Blake's works. There is less of the grotesque than in the others, and even more of the impressive. Much, however, depends upon the colouring, which varies greatly in different copies. Mr. Gilchrist warns us that it cannot be judged aright if we have not seen the "incomparable" copy in the possession of Lord Crewe. "It is printed in a warm reddish-brown, the exact colour of a very fine photograph ; and the broken blending of the deeper lines with the more tender shadows—all sanded over with a sort of golden mist peculiar to Blake's mode of execution—makes still more striking the resemblance to the then undiscovered handling of Nature herself." The general character of the design is excellently described by Gilchrist. "The subjects are vague and mystic as the poem itself. Female figures lie among waves full of reflected stars : a strange human image, with a swan's head and wings, floats on water in a kneeling attitude and drinks ; lovers embrace in an open water-lily ; an eagle-headed creature sits and contemplates the sun ; serpent-women are coiled with serpents ; Assyrian-looking, human-visaged bulls are seen yoked to the plough or the chariot ; rocks swallow or vomit forth human forms, or appear to amalgamate with them ; angels cross each other over wheels of flame ; and flames and hurrying figures wreathe and wind among the lines." It may indeed, like Blake's other productions of the kind, be described as a gigantic arabesque, imbued with a passion and pathos not elsewhere attempted in this branch of art.

The subject of *Milton*, from which one of our illustrations is selected,

Design from "Milton." By W. Blake.

is, in Mr. Swinburne's words, the incarnation and descent into earth and hell of Milton, who represents redemption by inspiration. Something similar, as we have seen, is the idea of Blake's fine mystical book, *Thel*, and the pilgrimage through a lower sphere is also found in the oldest Assyrian poetry. The book, like *Jerusalem*, is dated 1804, but, like its companion, must have been composed at Felpham. Nothing save actual and present contact with country scenes could have inspired such a passage as this, the crown of all Blake's unrhymed poetry :—

> Thou hearest the nightingale begin the song of spring :
> The lark sitting upon his earthly bed, just as the sun
> Appears, listens silent : then springing from the wavy corn-field loud
> He leads the choir of day : trill, trill, trill, trill :
> Mounting upon the wings of light into the great expanse ;
> Re-echoing against the lovely blue and shining heavenly shell :
> His little throat labours with inspiration, every feather
> On throat and breast and wings vibrates with the effluence divine :
> All nature listens silent to him, and the awful sun
> Stands still upon the mountain looking on this little bird
> With eyes of soft humility, and wonder, love, and awe.

Such a passage shows how greatly Blake might have gained as a poet had he been more intimate with external nature. Very splendid lines might be quoted from "Milton," such as "A cloudy heaven mingled with stormy seas in loudest ruin," but they are glowing light upon a black core of obscurity. Mr. Housman's judgment applies to it as to all the works of its class. "They are the sign chiefly of a beautiful nature wasted for lack of equipment in formulating disputatively what grew out of his better work with all the thoughtlessness and glory of a flower." [1]

Several lyrical poems printed in Blake's works may be assigned to this date. Some, such as "The Crystal Cabinet" and "The Mental Traveller," are extremely mystical ; others, such as "Mary," are of simply human interest ; others, such as "Auguries of Innocence," seem little remote from nonsense. "The Everlasting Gospel" expresses his profoundest ideas with startling crudity. None are wholly unmelodious,

[1] Blake is seldom detected in borrowing, but when he tells us that

> Milton's shadow fell
> Precipitant, loud thundering, into the sea of Time and space,

he is clearly, though perhaps unconsciously, reminiscent of Dyer's

> Towers
> Tumbling all precipitate down dashed,
> Rattling around, loud thundering to the Moon.

What time the thirteen Governors that England sent con-vene
In Bernards house; the flames coverd the land, they rouze they

Shaking their mental chains they rush in fury to the sea
To quench their anguish; at the feet of Washington down falln
They grovel on the sand and writhing lie: while all
The British soldiers thro' the thirteen states sent up a howl
Of anguish: threw their swords & muskets to the earth & ran
From their encampments and dark castles seeking where to hide
From the grim flames; and from the visions of Orc; in sight
Of Albions Angel; who enrag'd his secret clouds open'd
From north to south, and burnt outstretchd on wings of wrath covring
The eastern sky, spreading his awful wings across the heavens;
Beneath him roll'd his numrous hosts, all Albions Angels camp'd
Darkend the Atlantic mountains & their trumpets shook the valleys
Arm'd with diseases of the earth to cast upon the Abyss,
Their numbers forty millions, mustring in the eastern sky.

From Blake's "America."

but the old bewitching melody has gone from all, unless from the lines introductory to "Milton":—

> And did those feet in ancient time
> Walk upon England's mountains green;
> And was the holy Lamb of God
> On England's pleasant pastures seen?
>
> And did the countenance divine
> Shine forth upon our clouded hills?
> And was Jerusalem builded here
> Among these dark Satanic mills?
>
> Bring me my bow of burning gold,
> Bring me my arrows of desire:
> Bring me my spear: O clouds unfold!
> Bring me my chariot of fire!
>
> I will not cease from mental fight,
> Nor shall my sword sleep in my hand,
> Till we have built Jerusalem
> In England's green and pleasant land.

Blake, who had settled at 17, South Molton Street, Oxford Street, was in the meantime dealing with a very different patron from Hayley, Robert Cromek, a "stickit" engraver turned printseller, who tricked if he did not actually defraud him, but who is entitled to the credit of having recognised his genius, and of having brought forward works of his more adapted to attract public notice than anything he had yet done. These were the twelve illustrations to Blair's *Grave*, full of Blake's peculiar genius and at the same time intelligible to all. They had been executed in 1804 and 1805. Cromek, who afterwards admitted that they were worth sixty guineas, obtained them for twenty from the artist, who had intended to publish them himself. It had been understood that Blake should have engraved them, but Cromek, wisely from his own point of view, but wrongfully as regarded Blake, intrusted the task to Schiavonetti. As a frontispiece, they were accompanied by a portrait of Blake from a drawing by Phillips, also engraved by Schiavonetti, which we have reproduced. Thanks to Cromek's judicious engineering, and the popularity of the poem illustrated, the adventure proved a considerable success. "It is the only volume with Blake's name on the title-page," says Mr. Gilchrist, "which is not scarce." The publication took place in 1808.

Portrait of William Blake. From the engraving by L. Schiavonetti, after T. Phillips, R.A.

In the interval Cromek, calling upon Blake, had seen a pencil sketch of a design for the procession of Chaucer's Canterbury Pilgrims. Failing to obtain a finished drawing from the artist, who resented his previous treatment, he proposed the subject to Stothard, withholding as apart from all questions of Stothard's "frigid and exemplary" character would be most natural for him to do, all mention of Blake's drawing. Stothard accepted the commission; his elaborate oil picture was exhibited in 1807 with great success, but at the cost of a breach with Blake, who went so far in his denunciation, not only of Cromek's underhand dealing but of the defects which he found in Stothard's work, that when he afterwards sought a reconciliation Stothard remained impervious. Determined to vindicate his superiority, Blake completed, exhibited, and engraved his own fresco. The exhibition, accompanied by a remarkable "descriptive catalogue," to which we shall return—was not the success it might have been in the hands of the shrewd Cromek. The exhibition room was watched by Blake's brother James, whom Crabb Robinson asked whether he should be allowed to come again free in consideration of having bought four copies of the descriptive catalogue. "As long as you live," answered the overjoyed custodian. The success of the engraving was proportionate to that of the exhibition; though it might have been otherwise if the roughness of the original design had been smoothed down by the deft Schiavonetti. "Blake's production," says Mr. Rossetti, "is as unattractive as Stothard's is facile; as hard and strong as Stothard's is limp; one face in Blake's design means as much on the part of the artist, and takes as much scrutiny and turning over of thought on the part of the spectator, as all the pretty *fantoccini* and their sprightly little horses in Stothard's work." The engraving of the *Pilgrimage* in Gilchrist's biography evinces the justice of this criticism; though Ellis and Yeats rightly add that Blake has given all his personages the eyes of visionaries. "A work of wonderful power and spirit, hard and dry, yet with grace," says Charles Lamb. The original fresco was purchased by Elijah's raven, the ever-ready Butts.

We must now return to the illustrations to Blair's *Grave*, which are not only the most popular of Blake's works, but among his greatest. He showed in general more vigour in dealing with the conceptions of another than with his own, the latter imbibing an element of fanciful grace from the gentle spirit which produced them. Hence *The Soul*

Exploring the Recesses of the Grave, reproduced from *Thel*, though one of the most poetical of the designs, is one of the least powerful. His rendering of Blair's thoughts is marvellously direct and impressive, whether the passion depicted be joy, as in *The Reunion of the Soul and the Body* (given here), or horror, as in *The Death of the Strong Wicked Man*, or an intermediate shade, as in *The Soul hovering over the Body.* None of these and few of the series, once seen, will easily be forgotten. The most famous, and deservedly so, is the marvellous one, a combination of two designs in *America* and *The Gates of Paradise*, where the aged man, impelled by a strong wind, totters towards the portal of the sepulchre, on the summit of which sits the rejuvenated spirit, personified by a strong youth, rejoicing in his deliverance, but dazzled by the as yet unwonted light. In all these designs the element of seemly, yet slightly formal and conventional grace which Blake had learned from Stothard, is very conspicuous. The least successful, as seems to us, is *The Last Judgment*, where Blake appears as a minor Michael Angelo, but this work as engraved differs widely from his description of the work as exhibited. It may well be believed that the modified version was distinguished by great splendour of colouring.

Other works of this period were two small frescoes exhibited at the Academy in 1808, *Christ in the Sepulchre* and *Jacob's Dream*; the "ornamental device" engraved (by Cromek) along with the frontispiece to Malkin's *Father's Memoirs of his Child*, a graceful and pathetic composition; three illustrations to Shakespeare, one of which, the highly imaginative conception of the appearance of the Ghost to Hamlet, is engraved in Gilchrist's biography; *The Babylonian Woman on the Seven-headed Beast* (1809) reproduced here; a continuous series of designs produced for Mr. Butts, to be mentioned more fully hereafter; and the pictures displayed along with *The Canterbury Pilgrims* at its exhibition (1809). We must now devote some attention to Blake's appearance as an æsthetic writer in the *Descriptive Catalogue* he put forth on this occasion, with which his other principal deliverances on the subject of art may be advantageously grouped.

Blake's *Descriptive Catalogue* and his *Appeal to the Public* to judge between himself and his rivals in the department of engraving, are a singular mixture of gold and clay. The dignity which characterised his demeanour in life forsakes him as soon as he takes the pen into his hand,

The Reunion of Soul and Body. From Blair's "Grave," illustrated by W. Blake.

and he reviles Stothard, Woollett, and others in a strain inconsistent with self-respect on his own part, even had his criticism been well founded. As a matter of fact, it seems to have had no foundation, and assuredly has not affected the reputation of his antagonists in the smallest degree. At the same time it is impossible not to be moved by his earnestness. He is evidently contending for principles of great importance to himself, and through the mist of his confused and ungrammatical expression we seem to catch glimpses of high and serious truth. A refreshing contrast is afforded by the passages devoted to Chaucer, which are truly admirable for their felicitous insight into the old poet. "For all who have read Blake," justly say Messrs. Ellis and Yeats, "Chaucer is something more than the sweet spinner of rhyming gossip that he seems to most." Like Ruskin, and indeed all men of creative power, Blake is on much safer ground when he extols than when he censures. To much the same period belongs a remarkable paper on his *Last Judgment*, published by Gilchrist from his MS. Nothing of his admits us so fully into the sanctuary of his mind. "*The Last Judgment*," he begins, "is not fable or allegory, but vision. Fable, or allegory, is a totally distinct and inferior kind of poetry. Vision, or imagination, is a representation of what actually exists, really and unchangeably." Then follows an extremely graphic and vivid description of the painting, interspersed with profound remarks, such as "Man passes on, but states remain for ever; he passes through them like a traveller, who may as well suppose that the places he has passed through exist no more as a man may suppose that the states he has passed through exist no more; everything is eternal." "I have seen, when at a distance, multitudes of men in harmony appear like a single infant."[1] "In Hell all is self-righteousness; there is no such

[1] The same remark is the subject of one of the finest passages of Lucretius:—

Praeterea, magnae legiones quom loca cursu
Camporum complent, belli simulacra cientes,
Fulgur ibi ad cœlum se tollit, totaque circum
Aere renidescit tellus, subterque virum vi
Excitur pedibus sonitus, clamoreque montes
Icti rejectant voces ad sidera mundi;
Et circumvolitant equites, mediosque repente
Tramittunt, valido quatientes impete, campos;
Et tamen est quidam locus altis montibus, unde
Stare videntur, et in campis consistere fulgur.

The Babylonian Woman on the Seven-headed Beast. From a water-colour drawing by W. Blake. British Museum.

thing there as forgiveness of sin. He who does forgive sin is crucified as an abettor of criminals." "Angels are happier than men and devils, because they are not always prying after good and evil in one another, and eating the tree of knowledge for Satan's gratification." "*The Last Judgment* is an overwhelming of bad art and science." Finally, in words that state his own case as respects his reputed delusions, he says: "I assert for myself that I do not behold the outward creation, and that to me it is hindrance and not action. 'What!' it will be questioned, 'when the sun rises, do you not see a round disc of fire, somewhat like a guinea?' Oh! no! no! I see an innumerable company of the heavenly host, crying, 'Holy, holy, holy is the Lord God Almighty!' I question not my corporeal eye, any more than I would question a window concerning a sight. I look through it, and not with it."

Blake's conception of the sun may be compared with Dante's vision of the angels with the cloud:—

> Then lifting up mine eyes, as the tears came,
> I saw the Angels, like a rain of manna,
> In a long flight flying back heavenward;
> Having a little cloud in front of them,
> After the which they went, and said, "Hosanna!"
> And if they had said more, you should have heard.

An earlier acquaintance with Dante would undoubtedly have exerted a great influence upon Blake.

Not the least interesting part of Blake's catalogue is his description of the pictures accompanying his *Canterbury Pilgrims*, which include the strange patriotic allegories of *Nelson guiding Leviathan* and *Pitt guiding Behemoth*, the latter of which is now in the National Gallery; *Satan calling up his Legions; The Bard*, described by Rossetti as "a gorgeous piece of colour tone"; an idyll, charming in conception whatever it may have been in execution, representing goats nibbling the vine leaves that form the sole drapery of savage maidens; and Arthur's battle of Camlan, whence only three—the strongest, the most beautiful, and the ugliest of champions—escaped with their lives. This picture Seymour Kirkup thought Blake's best, and Allan Cunningham his worst. Kirkup, Mr. Swinburne tells us, remembered to the last "the fury and splendour of energy there contrasted with the serene ardour of simply beautiful courage, the violent life of the design, and the fierce distance of fluctuating battle." Blake's estimate of his powers, as conveyed in his descriptions of his works, certainly does not err on the side of modesty; perhaps he thought with Goethe that "Nur die Lumpen sind bescheiden." It is a more serious matter that the descriptions are crammed with statements far more significant than Blake's visions of a condition of mental disorder, such as that the Greek marbles are copies of the works of the Asiatic patriarchs; that no one painted in oil, except by accident, before Vandyke; that ancient British heroes dwell to this day on Snowdon "in naked simplicity": a species of Welsh Mahatmas, as it would appear. It would have been a judicious emendation if any one had suggested the substitution of "lying spirits" when the artist spoke of himself as "molested by blotting and blurring demons."

More important than these idle extravagances, though extravagant enough, are the annotations on Reynolds's discourses, written a few years afterwards. To read Blake's abuse of this great artist with any patience, one must remember that his expressions require to be translated out of his peculiar dialect into ordinary speech; as when, for example, he says that Correggio is a most effeminate and cruel demon, he only means that he is a bad model for artists to follow. Yet there is a great and serious truth lying at the bottom of Blake's declamation, and his protest against the apparent tendency of Reynolds to inculcate the feasibility of manufacturing genius by study was not uncalled for. What he did not sufficiently remember was that the number of artists capable of what Plato calls divine insanity, must always be very small, and that Reynolds's precepts may be very serviceable for the rank and file of the great army. As his denunciation of Reynolds was partly prompted by personal grievances (not the less real, if the apparent paradox may be excused, for being imaginary), it is the more to his honour to find him breaking out into genuine admiration whenever, in Swedenborg's phrase, the dry rod blossoms as Reynolds affirms a truth. It is also pleasant to receive Samuel Palmer's assurance that Blake's splenetic outbreaks in print astonished those accustomed to his catholicity of criticism in conversation.

CHAPTER IV

Blake's Life in South Molton Street and Fountain Court—Acquaintance with Linnell and Varley—Drawings of Visionary Heads—Miscellaneous Works in Private Collections—Illustrations of "Job"—Work as an Engraver—Acquaintance with Crabb Robinson—Illustrations of Dante—Declining health and death—General observations—His principal Biographer and Critics.

VERY little is known of Blake's life for several years after his exhibition. William Carey, a rare example of disinterestedness among picture-dealers, for he praised Blake enthusiastically without having dealt with him, says in his exposition of West's *Death on the Pale Horse* (1817), "So entire is the uncertainty in which he is involved that after many inquiries I meet with some in doubt whether he is still in existence. But I have accidentally learned since I commenced these remarks that he is now a resident in London." He was, in fact, continuing to live on his second floor in South Molton Street, poor, but content, subsisting from day to day by hack work as an engraver, and the occasional sale of a water-colour design or a coloured copy of one of his books, but nowise squalid, abject, or destitute. He was no longer able to publish on his own account as of old, and the poems which he continued to produce abundantly, all of which have perished, met with the reception which was to be expected from earthly publishers. Blake smiled in pity, assured that, in his own figurative language, they were handsomely printed and bound in heaven, and eagerly perused by spiritual intelligences. "I should be sorry," he afterwards said to Crabb Robinson, "if I had any earthly fame, for whatever natural glory a man has is so much taken from his spiritual glory." He certainly had not thought so when he published his catalogue; but there is no question of his perfect sincerity when he added, "I wish to do nothing for profit. I wish to live for art." Though he had said "Thought is act: Christ's acts were nothing to Cæsar's if this is not so";

so intense was his own devotion to labour that for two years he never quitted his lodging, except (for the ridiculous will intrude where it is not wanted—imps grin in the cells of anchorites—) for a pot of porter Even while he engraved he read, as the plate-marks on his books attest. Flaxman, his steady friend from youth, found him some work in engraving, and praised him in conversation. "But Blake's a wild enthusiast, isn't he?" "Some think *me* an enthusiast," answered Flaxman, who was, in truth, more than half a Swedenborgian.

From this hermit's existence Blake once more emerges, in 1818, into comparative publicity through the intimacy he formed with a young painter of promise, which he was destined to more than redeem. This was John Linnell, who was introduced to him by Mr. George Cumberland, of Bristol, an enlightened patron of art. At this time Linnell was largely engaged in portrait painting, and the plate of the portrait selected here for reproduction, that of Wilson Lowry, Esq., appears to have been worked upon by both him and Blake, bearing the name of each. Linnell, though neither gentle nor mystical, lived much in the world of the spirit, and, without sharing Blake's peculiarities, was rather attracted than repelled by them. Within a few days after making Blake's acquaintance he had found him work to the amount of fifteen guineas, and gradually introduced him to patrons, including Sir Thomas Lawrence, a great gentleman as well as a fine painter, who took the notice of Blake which it became him to take in his position as President of the Royal Academy. Blake never encountered hostility from artists of true eminence. Reynolds advised him wisely, though he would not think so. Lawrence patronised him; and Flaxman, Fuseli, Stothard, Linnell were, so far as he permitted them, real friends. Within a few years Linnell had introduced him to a younger circle, ready in a measure to sit at his feet, and the rejected stone was honourably built into the corner. Of these we shall have to speak afterwards, but one important intimacy mainly belongs to the period of 1818–21. This was his acquaintance with John Varley, famed as one of the fathers of English water-colour painting, but even more renowned as an astrologer. Indeed, some of the stories told of his successful predictions are less startling to the uninitiated than to astrologers themselves, who cannot comprehend on what principle of the art they could be made. They certainly were not arrived at by vision or revelation, for the good Varley was a most unspiritual personage, the very antipodes of seer or anchorite, big, sanguine, jovial, and everlastingly in the claws of the bailiffs. Astrology, therefore, a study which, with all its fascination for an imaginative mind, requires nothing but observation and calculation, was the only occult science open to him ; for magic, although a diabolical pursuit, occasionally demands an amount of fasting inconvenient even for a saint. Varley would have wished to go further, and finding the perception of visions inconsistent with his own corporeal and spiritual constitution, was delighted to make the acquaintance of one who to this end needed but to open his eyes. He speedily developed the practical idea that Blake should depict the spiritual entities which he beheld. Blake forthwith set to work, and ere long the portfolios of Varley and Linnell were enriched with those ghosts of fleas, portraits of Edward the Third, and men who built the pyramids, which are better known to many than anything he ever did, and are assuredly no mean examples of his imaginative power. "All," says Gilchrist, "are marked by a decisive portrait-like character, and are evidently literal portraits of what Blake's imaginative eye beheld." [1] This is corroborated by the account of Varley, who says, "On hearing of this spiritual apparition of a Flea, I asked him if he could draw for me the resemblance of what he saw. He instantly said, 'I see him now before me.' I therefore gave him a paper and a pencil, with which he drew the portrait of which a facsimile is given in this number [of Varley's *Zodiacal Physiognomy*]. I felt convinced by his mode of proceeding that he had a real image before him ; for he left off and began on another part of the paper to make a separate drawing of the mouth of the Flea, which the spirit having opened he was prevented from proceeding with the first sketch till he had closed it." It was "an idea with the force of a sensation," as Peacock's philosopher classifies the apparition in *Nightmare Abbey*. Shelley, who also saw visions, has enriched his note-books with similar delineations of imaginary figures, generally vague and careless, but sometimes very Blake-like. One of Linnell's most spirited studies from life, engraved in Story's biography, represents Blake and Varley in discussion.

[1] Not always without assistance from the eyes of others ; for the portrait of Edward the First is clearly a reminiscence of that which in Blake's time adorned Goldsmith's History.

These drawings were mostly executed in 1819 and 1820. In the latter year Blake lost his chief patron Butts, whose walls, indeed, had become so crowded with his works that he had almost ceased to give him

Portrait of Wilson Lowry. By John Linnell. Engraved by Blake and Linnell.

commissions. The greater part of the collection was dispersed in 1852, but the zeal of Mr. W. M. Rossetti traced most of its constituents out, and reference to his notes, printed in the second volume of Gilchrist's biography, will enable us to convey some faint notion of its manifold opulence. Putting the *Job* aside for the present, the most remarkable appear to be the nine designs for *Paradise Lost*, the property of Mr. J. C. Strange, in which, says Mr. Rossetti, Blake is king of all his powers of design, draughtsmanship, conception, spiritual meaning, and impression. Another set, belonging to Mr. Aspland, of Liverpool, omits one subject and adds four. Another set of Miltonic designs for *Comus*, rather distinguished by grace than grandeur, has been recently published by Mr. Quaritch. Another set of no less than one hundred and eighteen designs for Gray's works, in 1860 in the possession of the Duke of Hamilton, are reputed to rank among Blake's finest productions, but have not been inspected by any one competent to describe them. Among others especially commended by Mr. Rossetti are *The Sacrifice of Jephthah's Daughter*, *Ruth*, *The Judgment of Paris*, *The Wise and Foolish Virgins*, *Fire*, *Famine*, *Samson subdued*, *The Finding of Moses*, *Moses erecting the Brazen Serpent*, *The Ghost of Samuel appearing to Saul*, *The Entombment*, *The Sealing of the Sepulchre*, *The Angel rolling the Stone from the Sepulchre*, *The River of Life*, and *Hecate*. To these may be added *The Resurrection of the Dead*, now in the British Museum, reproduced by us. Many others, not belonging to the Butts collection, are described with equal enthusiasm ; and, apart from all questions of technical execution, usually splendid, but lost upon those who have not access to the original works, it may be said that the conceptions, as described by Mr. Rossetti, would be impossible to one unendowed with the highest artistic imagination, and that the body is worthy of the spirit.

Prominent among these designs are the set of illustrations to *Job*, now the property of the Earl of Crewe. A duplicate set belonged to Mr. Linnell, who, "discounting as it were," says Gilchrist, "Blake's bill on posterity when no one else would," commissioned this from him, tracing the outlines from Butt's copy himself, and handing them over to Blake to complete. This was done in September, 1821, and when the drawings were completed in 1823 Linnell went further still, and commissioned Blake to engrave them, a stroke which has probably effected more than anything else for the artist's fame, for the drawings which have set him on such a pinnacle, if unengraved, would have remained virtually unknown to the world. The terms also were liberal. Blake was to receive £100 for the twenty-two plates and £100 more out of the profits.

The Resurrection of the Dead. From a water-colour drawing by W. Blake.
British Museum.

When the publication barely covered its expenses, Linnell, reflecting that the plates remained in his possession in virtue of the agreement, not unreasonably but very handsomely allowed Blake £50 more. But for this manna from heaven Blake's last years would have been spent in engraving pigs and poultry after Morland. Linnell, who was himself an excellent engraver, further conferred an important benefit upon him by making him acquainted with the best style of Italian engraving. Blake proved a docile pupil at sixty-five, and his plates to *Job* are not only technically the best he ever executed, but occupy an important place in the history of the art.

The glory of *Job*, however, is not in the engraving, but in the invention, which, beautiful in the soft and idyllic passages, rises into sublimity when the theme appeals strongly to the creative imagination. It is especially remarkable as being one of the very few instances of a worthy representation of the Almighty. The tender humanities of Christian art are absent: all is awful, Hebraic, and strictly monotheistic. Among the most remarkable designs may be noted that where the exulting fiend pulls down the mansion upon Job's sons and daughters (reproduced here); the frantic speed of the messenger of evil, who bursts out with his tale before he is well within hearing, while another follows with equal haste hard upon him, and the uninterested sheep graze on undisturbed; the terrible scene where Satan, a figure repeated in essentials from works of earlier date, smites the prostrate Job with sore boils; Eliphaz besieged with phantoms, to all seeming not less real than himself (also given here); the morning stars singing together; the downfall of the wicked; and the Lord answering Job out of the whirlwind. Passages even of the less striking designs often have a singular fascination, such as the night-piercing stars in the Elihu scene, which would be impressive in the absence of any human figure; Behemoth and Leviathan, the *ne plus ultra* of grotesque grandeur, which we have also given; and the bowed backs of Job's accusing friends when the Lord blesses him.[1] On the whole,

[1] It is observable that Job's wife, so disadvantageously treated in Scripture, is by Blake represented as the sufferer's loving companion throughout. This was probably out of tenderness to Mrs. Blake, from whom, indeed, upon a comparison between her portrait as a young woman and the ideal representation of the Patriarch's spouse, his model for the latter would seem to have been derived; but if so the inference seems justified that Blake regarded the story of Job as emblematic of his own history.

though others of Blake's designs may be more transcendent of ordinary human faculty, he has scarcely executed anything displaying all his faculties so well combined and in such perfect equilibrium ; and, were it necessary to rest his fame upon one set of works, this would probably be selected. As a scriptural theme it appealed with especial strength to English sympathies, and having been selected by Gilchrist for reproduction, it is more widely known than any of his works except the illustrations to Blair's *Grave*. "The original water-colour designs," Rossetti says, "are much larger than the engravings, and generally pale in colour, with a less full and concentrated effect than the engravings, and by no means equal to them in power and splendid decorative treatment of the light and shade. On the other hand, they are often completer and naturally freer in expression, and do not exhibit a certain tendency to over-sturdiness of build and physiognomy in the figures." Fine as is the .gure of Satan in *The Destruction of Job's Sons and Daughters*, it is, Mr. Rossetti thinks, much finer in the water colour. On the other hand, "the effect of sublimity and multitude in *When the morning stars sang together* is centupled in the engraving by adding the upraised arms of two other angels to right and left, passing out of the composition." The whole account suggests how desirable it would be to have many of Blake's unpublished water colours translated into black and white, could engraver or etcher of the needful force be found.

Woodcut from Thornton's Pastoral.

In 1821 Blake had performed another work of moment, his first and last wood - engravings. These were to illustrate Phillips's imitation of Virgil's first pastoral, republished by Dr. Thornton, a physician and botanist. Blake was a novice in this branch of art, and the cuts answer to Dr. Thornton's own description of them : "They display less of art than of genius." But nothing could more effectually confirm the principle enunciated by their critic in the *Athenæum* : "Amid all drawbacks there exists a power in the work of the man of genius which no one but himself can utter fully." Rude as they are, their force is extraordinary; few things can be more truly magical than the glimpse of distant sea in the second of those engraved by Gilchrist. At the same time they are not in the least Virgilian, and in this respect form an instructive contrast with the exquisite though unfinished Virgilian illustrations of Samuel Palmer. Palmer, though putting in a cypress now and then as a tribute to *couleur locale*, provides Virgil substantially with the same style of illustration as he had been producing all his life for other ends, and yet this seems as appropriate to the text as Blake's is discrepant. It is interesting to speculate what effect an Italian residence of two or three years, such as Palmer had enjoyed, would have produced upon Blake beyond the inevitable one of dissipating his monstrous delusions about Italian artists. He would probably have gone chiefly with the view of studying Michael Angelo, but we suspect that the influences of Italian landscape would in the long run have proved fully as potent.

In 1821 Blake removed from South Molton Street to Fountain Court, Strand, near the Savoy, where he occupied two rooms on the first floor. The reason may have been that the house was kept by a brother-in-law of Mrs. Blake's named Baines, the only trace we have of any connection with his wife's family. Economy too may have had its influence; his means were very low, not yet improved by the donation of £25 he received from the Academy next year, or his arrangement with Linnell in the year following. At the worst, however, the rooms were always clean and neat, thanks to Mrs. Blake's industry and devotion; and Blake's manner always had the simplicity and dignity of a gentleman. That his circumstances improved was almost entirely the doing of Linnell, who not only provided for his wants by commissions, but made him what his genius had never made him, the patriarch of a band of admirers, almost disciples. Coming frequently to visit Linnell at Hampstead, Blake fell in with a group of young men who resorted thither, four of whom at least—Samuel Palmer, Edward Calvert, George Richmond, and F. O. Finch—became artists of great distinction. One characteristic these young men had in common: they were as far as possible from the theory of art for art's sake, but only valued art as the outward and visible sign of the inward and spiritual grace of consecration to the Power behind Nature. The biographies of Palmer and Calvert disclose the priestlike spirit in which they wrought, a spirit akin to that of their pre-Raphaelite successors, but apparently less impregnated with the ordinary atmosphere of the studio. These were just the men to treat the aged Blake as the

The Destruction of Job's Sons and Daughters. From the "Book of Job." By W. Blake.

antediluvian youth ought to have treated the aged Jubal; and the patriarchal influence is visible both in their writings and their works, not always to the advantage of the latter, if we may judge by the examples preserved of Palmer's early labours. But all seemed fair in the light of fond retrospect. Twenty-eight years after Blake's death Samuel Palmer addressed a letter to Mr. Gilchrist, long and full of interesting particulars relating to Blake's opinions on art ; but the gist of the estimate of the man is conveyed in few words. "In him you saw at once the Maker, the Inventor ; one of the few in any age ; a fitting companion for Dante. He was energy itself, and shed around him a kindling influence, an atmosphere of life, full of the ideal. He was a man without a mask ; his aim single, his path straightforwardness, and his wants few ; so he was free, noble, and happy."

A very important witness to Blake's demeanour and opinions in his later years is Henry Crabb Robinson the diarist, whom we have already met as a visitor to Blake's exhibition, and who had made him the subject of an essay in a German periodical. Robinson was the right man in the right place, not being a mystic or enthusiast to fall down at Blake's feet, nor yet a man of the world to deride him as a visionary, but an inquisitive observer of great intellectual range and most kindly and tolerant disposition, ready to allow that things might exist of which his philosophy had not dreamed, and whom abnormal opinions, if held in evident sincerity, might startle but could hardly shock. "It is strange," says he, "that I who have no imagination, nor any power beyond that of a logical understanding, should yet have a great respect for religious mystics." Thrown into Blake's company in 1825, he has recorded his conversations with him at considerable length in his delightful diary, as yet but partially published. His description of Blake's "interesting appearance" agrees with that of his own circle. "He is pale, with a Socratic countenance, and an expression of great sweetness, though with something of languor about it except when animated, and then he has about him an air of inspiration. The tone and manner are incommunicable. There are a natural sweetness and gentility about him which are delightful." Having heard of Blake's visions, Robinson was not surprised to find him asserting that the visionary gift was innate in all men, and only torpid for want of cultivation ; but he must have had much ado to digest such statements as that the world was flat, that Wordsworth was a Pagan, and that "what are called the vices in the natural world are the highest sublimities in the spiritual world." Not understanding that by atheism

Blake meant, in his own words, "whatever assumes the reality of the natural and unspiritual world," Robinson was naturally aghast when Locke was classed with atheists, and ventured what must have appeared to him the conclusive rejoinder that Locke had written in defence of Christianity. Blake, who probably understood Robinson's definition of atheism as little as Robinson did his, "made no reply." Some of Blake's remarks are well worthy of preservation. "Art is inspiration. When Michael

With Dreams upon my Bed thou scarest me. From the "Book of Job." By W. Blake.

Angelo, or Raphael, or Mr. Flaxman does any of his fine things, he does them in the spirit." "Irving is a *sent* man. But they who are sent go further sometimes than they ought." "Dante saw devils where I see none."

Dante must have been much in Blake's thoughts just then, for Robinson found him occupied with the long series of illustrations of the poet commissioned by Linnell, the last important work of his life. The history of the commission is thus related by Linnell's biographer, Mr. Story. "Although the *Job* had been paid for, Linnell continued to give him money weekly. Blake said, 'I do not know how I shall ever repay you.' Linnell replied, 'I do not want you to repay me. I am only too glad to be able to serve you. What I would like, however, if you do anything for me, is that you should make some designs for Dante's *Inferno*, *Purgatorio*, and *Paradiso*.' Blake entered upon the work with alacrity, concurrently with the engraving of the *Job* designs, and the two together occupied the old man for the rest of his life." During all this period Linnell was remitting Blake money, as the latter's notes in acknowledgment prove. Linnell undoubtedly acquired the designs at a low price, but immediately upon Blake's death he endeavoured to dispose of them for the benefit of the widow. Failing in this he kept them, never attempting to make anything by them; and they are still in the possession of his family.

Blake studied Italian to qualify himself more effectually for his task, and is said to have acquired it; when Robinson saw him, however, at an early stage of the commission it is true, he was working by the aid of Cary's English version. He executed no less than ninety-eight drawings, several of which were left in an unfinished state. Seven have been engraved. The merits of the series have been variously estimated. Mr. Rossetti considers them "on the whole a very fine series, though not uniformly equal in merit." Mr. Yeats, so well qualified by his own imaginative gift to enter into the merit of Blake's work, thinks them the finest of all his productions. Robinson, who saw Blake at work upon them, says, "They evince a power I should not have anticipated of grouping, and of throwing grace and interest over conceptions monstrous and horrible." For our own part, we must regretfully admit that when we saw them at the Old Masters' exhibition the monstrosity and horror appeared more evident than the grace and interest. We could not deem Dante's conceptions adequately rendered; the colour, too, often seemed harsh and extravagant. Blake went on working upon them until his death, when Mrs. Blake sent them to Linnell. They thus escaped the fate of Blake's other artistic and literary remains left in his widow's possession, which after her death were appropriated, apparently without any legal authority, by a person named Tatham, who had been much about

Blake in his later years, and who ultimately destroyed them in deference to the mandate of a religious sect with which he had become connected ![1]

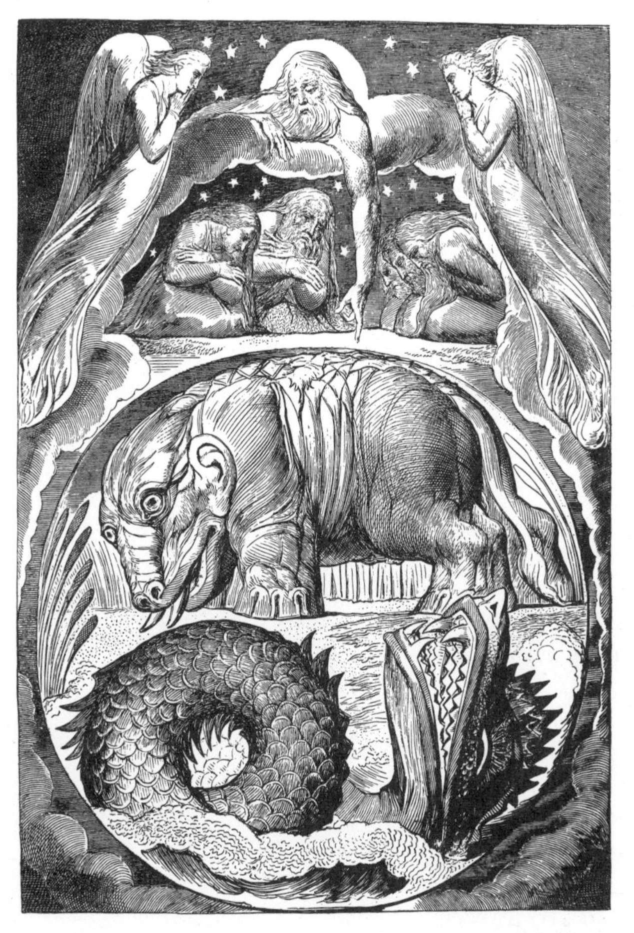

Behemoth and Leviathan. From the "Book of Job." By W. Blake.

[1] It must be now about thirty-five years since we received a visit from this person ; how he had found us out we cannot recollect. He stated that he had lived by painting miniatures, and, having been deprived of his customers by photography, proposed to

The end was now near. During 1827 Blake's health greatly failed from catarrh and dysentery, and he could no longer go up to Hampstead to see Linnell. Linnell wished him to quit the damp neighbourhood of the river, and live in his own house in Cirencester Place, part only of which he used as a studio. But Blake said, "I cannot get my mind out of a state of terrible fear at such a step." He also said, "I am too much attached to Dante to think much of anything else." One of his last works was the colouring of *The Ancient of Days* for the elder Tatham, who paid him at a higher rate than he was accustomed to receive. Blake accordingly worked his hardest, and when it was finished "threw it from him, and with an air of exulting triumph exclaimed, 'There, that will do, I cannot mend it.'" Later still he exclaimed to his wife, "You have ever been an angel to me, I will draw you," and produced a sketch, "interesting, but not like." On August 12 he died, "composing and uttering songs to his Maker." He was buried in Bunhill Fields, in a grave which cannot now be identified. It is little to the honour of his countrymen that no public memorial of him should exist. A better one could not be than his own *Death's Door* in the illustration to Blair's *Grave*, treated as a bas-relief with the necessary modifications.

The artist whose life had been spent in a condition so little remote from penury did not leave a single debt, and the accumulated stock of his works sufficed to support his widow in comfort for the four years for which she survived him. Friends, indeed, aided, Linnell and Tatham successively giving her house-room, and others assiduously recommending her stores of drawings to wealthy patrons. She died in Upper Charlotte Street, Fitzroy Square, and was buried beside her husband in Bunhill Fields.

The artistic processes used by Blake are a subject of considerable discussion. Notwithstanding his constant description of his pictures as

devote himself to historical painting, to the great prospective advantage of British art. He considered his forte to be the delineation of bare arms, and wished to be recommended to a subject which would afford scope for the exercise of this department of the pictorial faculty. We suggested the interment of the young princes in the Tower; he thanked us and departed; and we saw no more of him. He admitted having parted with all the relics of Blake that had been in his possession, but sought to convey that they had been sold, not destroyed, which may be partly true.

"frescoes," it seems certain that he never resorted to fresco in the ordinary acceptation of the term. Linnell, who must have been exceedingly familiar with his work, told Mr. Gilchrist: "He evidently founded his claim to the name fresco on the material he used, which was water-colour on a plaster ground (literally glue and whiting); but he always called it either fresco, gesso, or plaster." Linnell added that when he himself obtained from Italy the first copy that ever came to England of Cennino Cennini's *Trattato della Pittura*, a sixteenth-century treatise, edited in 1822 from the original MS., Blake, who was soon able to read it, "was gratified to find that he had been using the same materials and methods in painting as Cennini describes, particularly the carpenter's glue." "Unfortunately," says Linnell, "he laid this ground on too much like plaster to a wall," and when this was so applied to canvas or linen the picture was sure to crack, and many of Blake's best works have suffered great injury. Oil he disliked and vituperated. The reason probably was that, contrary to what might have been expected, his system of execution was by no means bold and dashing, but deliberate and even slow. He drew a rough dotted line with pencil, then with ink, then colour, filling in cautiously and carefully. All the grand efforts of design, he thought, depended on niceties not to be got at once. He seems, in fact, to have worked very much in the spirit of the mediæval illuminators, and the general aspect of a page of one of his Prophetical Books reminds us forcibly of one of their scrolls. Whether any direct influence from them upon him is traceable would be difficult to determine. Keats had evidently seen illuminated manuscripts, and been deeply impressed by them; but nearly forty years elapsed between the publication of the first of Blake's Prophetical Books and the composition of Keats's *Eve of St. Mark*. In one respect Blake certainly differed from the ancient miniaturists; he wrought mainly from reminiscence, and disliked painting with his eye on the object. His memory for natural forms must have been very powerful.

Blake is endowed in a very marked degree with the interest ascribed by Goethe to *Problematische Naturen*, men who must always remain more or less of a mystery to their fellows. In ancient times, and perhaps in some countries at the present day, he would have been accepted as a seer; in his own age and country the question was rather whether he should be classed with visionaries or with lunatics. A visionary he certainly was, and few will believe either that his visions had any objective reality, or that he himself intended them to be received merely as symbols. "You can see what I do, if you choose," he said to his friends. He thus confused fancy with fact; unquestionably, therefore, he laboured under delusions. But delusions do not necessarily amount to insanity, and, however Blake erred in form, it may be doubted whether in essentials he was not nearer the truth than most so-called poets and artists. Every poet and artist worthy of the name will confess that his productions, when really good for anything, are the suggestion of a power external to himself, of an influence which he may to a certain extent guide, but cannot originate or summon up at his will; and in the absence of which he is helpless. In personifying this influence as the Muse, or howsoever he may prefer to describe it, such an one is usually fully aware that, in obedience to a law of the human mind, he is bestowing personality and visibility upon what is actually invisible and impersonal, but not on that account unreal. Some there are, however, whose perceptions are so lively, or their power of dealing with abstractions so limited, that the mental influences of which they are conscious appear to them in the light of personalities. Such was Blake, and the peculiarity in him was probably closely connected with the childlike disposition which rendered him so amiable as a man. As a child it naturally never occurred to him to question the reality of his visions, and he grew up without acquiring the critical habit of mind which would have led him to do so. With him "the vision splendid" did *not*

> Die away,
> And fade into the light of common day.

Such a state of mind is quite compatible with sanity. The question is not whether the person

> Gives to airy nothings
> A local habitation and a name,

but whether he allows his conduct to be actuated by them to the extent of inverting the rules of right and wrong, wasting his substance, or becoming offensive to others or dangerous to himself. It is even possible to travel far in this direction without arriving at the confines of insanity.

Prince Polignac brought the monarchy of the Restoration to ruin in deference to imaginary revelations from the Virgin Mary, yet no court of law would ever have placed him under restraint. With Blake not the faintest suggestion of such a thing is possible. Except for one or two incidents, related upon doubtful authority, he appears throughout his life in the light of an exemplary citizen, and in his unselfishness and unworldliness contrasts with his Sadducæan neighbours in a way that forbids us to call him mentally diseased, though he may have been mentally warped. The value of his mystical utterances is quite another question. The occasional splendour of the poetry in which they are couched will not be disputed, any more than their general confusion and obscurity. Commentators have striven hard to elicit the sunbeam from the cucumber ; we pass no judgment on their efforts, further than may seem to be implied in the observation that in our opinion the chief mission of Blake's mystical poetry was to be the vehicle of his finest and most characteristic art. His ideas, many profound and worthy of close attention, may, we think, be more advantageously collected from his prose aphorisms and the fragments of his conversation ; and in this respect he is by no means singular. The one great achievement which unquestionably entitles him to the distinction of an inspired man, is to have produced in boyhood, without set purpose or any clear consciousness of what he was doing, lyrics recalling the golden prime of English poetry, and instinct with a music to which, since Chatterton was no more, no contemporary save Burns was capable of making the slightest approach. It is true that reaction against artifice and conventionality was in the air of the time, and was already announced by evident symptoms. To compare, however, the highly creditable efforts in this direction of even such poets as Cowper and Mickle with the achievements of this stripling is to become sensible at once of the difference between talent and inspiration.

Blake's gifts and shortcomings as an artist are sufficiently revealed by the examples of his work which accompany this essay. It need merely be remarked here that, apart from the great army of artists of genius who move on recognised lines, transmitting the succession from the age of Zeuxis and Phidias to our own, there is, as it were, a parallel column skirting it on the by-roads of art ; and that at certain periods of Art's history the genius which has forsaken the more conspicuous of her manifestations has seemed to take refuge with etchers, or designers, or delineators of the life of the people. It has frequently happened of late that men whose work was chiefly done for books and periodicals, and who during their lives were scarcely regarded as artists at all, have upon their deaths been deservedly exalted to very high places. Blake is perhaps the most striking and remarkable example of this class.

Blake's peculiarities as a man, and the anecdotes of which he became the subject, secured him earlier attention as artist and poet than his works would have obtained on their own account. Not long after his death he was made (1830) the subject of one of Allan Cunningham's *Lives of British Painters*, in the main a fair and impartial biography, rather in advance of than behind its time. Cunningham, however, possessed no sort of spiritual kinship with Blake, who found his first really congenial commentator in a veteran philosopher, still happily spared to us, Dr. James Garth Wilkinson, who in 1839, the year of the first collected edition of Shelley's poems, republished *Songs of Innocence and Experience* with an anonymous preface claiming for Blake something like his proper position as a lyric poet, and accompanied by judicious remarks upon his paintings. Dr. Wilkinson would probably have expressed himself still more decidedly if he had written a few years later, but the movement towards the exaltation of the more spiritual aspects of English poetry as typified in Wordsworth and Shelley was as yet but incipient, and the stars of Tennyson and Browning were hardly above the horizon. Little further seems to have been done for Blake, until, about 1855, the late Mr. Alexander Gilchrist began to write his biography, published in 1862, a labour of love and diligence which will never be superseded, especially since the revision it has received in the definitive edition of 1880, brought out by his widow. The value of Gilchrist's labours is greatly enhanced by the accompanying illustrations, which allow a fairly adequate conception to be formed of Blake's pictorial genius, by the reprint of much of his most characteristic literary work, and by the copious descriptions of his drawings by Mr. W. M. Rossetti and Mr. F. Shields. Since Gilchrist wrote, Mr. Swinburne (1868) has investigated Blake's thought with special reference to its Pantheistic tendency, and Messrs. Ellis and Yeats, in a most comprehensive work in three volumes (1891), including additional biographical particulars and copious illustrations, which comprise the previously unpublished "Vala," have striven to present Blake's mysticism as a coherent system of thought. Valuable monographs are also prefixed to the editions of Blake's poems by Rossetti (1883) and Yeats (1893), and to the selection from his literary works by Mr. Housman (1893), this last perhaps on the whole, after Gilchrist's biography, the most desirable possession for the literary student of Blake. Of the numerous detached essays upon Blake the most important, perhaps, are that by the late Mr. Smetham, republished in his Essays, and in the second volume of Gilchrist's biography, and that by James Thomson, author of *The City of Dreadful Night*, appended to his *Shelley, a Poem* (1884).

It is exceedingly difficult to obtain a proper idea of Blake as an artist, from the extent to which his designs depend upon colouring, and the great inequality of this colouring, which is often not his own. In Mr. Gilchrist's opinion, the copy of *The Song of Los*, in the Print Room of the British Museum, and a volume of miscellaneous designs, in the same collection, represent him with adequate fairness; and these fortunately are public property. The finest specimens of his work seen by his biographer are apparently in the collection of the Earl of Crewe, and therefore not generally accessible. Those belonging to private collectors must of necessity be continually changing hands, and few students have the time or the opportunity to make the thorough investigation of them accomplished by Mr. Rossetti. Fortunately the illustrations in Gilchrist's biography, where the whole of the *Job* series is reissued, suffice to establish Blake's genius as a designer, even though destitute of the charm of colour. Mr. Bell Scott has executed effective etchings after him; Mr. Quaritch has republished the drawings for *Comus*; in 1876 the *Songs of Innocence and Experience* and the Prophetic Books up to *Los* were reprinted together, but only to the extent of a hundred copies, nor was the execution very satisfactory. It cannot be said that Messrs. Ellis and Yeats have entirely overcome the difficulties of reproduction; yet, perhaps, for those unable to obtain access to the copies tinted by the artist, or even to the uncoloured plates in the original edition, nothing so well displays the wilder and more weird aspects of his genius as the reprints in their third volume, especially those from *Jerusalem*.

Blake's character and works will long remain the subject of criticism and speculation, for the world does not easily forgo its interest in what Goethe calls "problematic natures." By another famous saying of Goethe's he cannot profit, "He who has sufficed his own age has sufficed all ages," nor can he be reckoned among those who have been in advance of their age, except in those exquisite early songs which died away before the actual arrival of the better time. But it would not be too much to say of him that he revealed possibilities, both in poetry and painting, which without him we should hardly have suspected, and which remain an unexhausted seed-field of inspiration for his successors. It is labour lost to strive to make him transparent, but even where he is most opaque

> Sparks spring out of the ground,
> Like golden sand scattered upon the darkness.

Nor is the general tendency of art towards a world of purity, harmony, and joy unrepresented in him; sometimes this even seems the conclusion to which all else is merely subservient, as in the series of illustrations to Job, the ideal representation of his own history.

Sweeping the Parlour in the Interpreter's House.

INDEX